A Warrior's Tale

A Warrior's Tale

A true story of a near death experience and return

Tommie Little, Esquire

Library of Congress Control Number:		2009909593
ISBN:	Hardcover	978-1-4415-8021-4
	Softcover	978-1-4415-8020-7

This book was printed in the United States of America.

To order additional copies of this book, contact:
Xlibris Corporation
1-888-795-4274
www.Xlibris.com
Orders@Xlibris.com

67743

Dedication

This book is for **WARRIORS**
This book is for **myself**
This book is for my **family**
This book is for my **friends**
This book is for my **enemies**
OORAH!

Introduction

I have been back in my home country the good ol' US of A from my African wanderings and adventures around 4 years . . . no one ever says . . . How was Africa? I am only reminded of my 12 year meanderings by occasional Discovery or Travel channels . . . . but it ain't the same. Five weeks ago, I was moving a box from my storage closet and a yellowed old News Journal article fell at my feet . . . a sharp corner hit my bare toe with force, I pay attention to things like that, when you read this story you'll know exactly why???

I bent to pick it up . . . the 10 year old headline blared . . . "Ex Wilmington Lawyer lands on his feet". I shook my head and wondered what the hell ever happened to that old man from Delaware who died in the deadly cerebral malaria epidemic in a bush hospital and then came back after four days to talk about it . . . Well, I haven't talked about it for years and swore I never would again . . . that is, until the article landed on my foot.

I was pushed immediately and directly to the key board of my computer as if something had me by the back of my neck and I typed for five straight weeks. After the first Chapter was written, I decided it was a good story and I sent it out as an email to my Delaware First Responder Community. a group I formed to launch America's First Homeland Security Charter School. For many years this email community kept me safe and sane by putting up with my barrage of email's for all my goofy public interest projects as the very charitable warriors that they are.

One guy in our community, Judson Bennett, my close personal friend and regular political adversary sent it to 5000 members of his COASTAL CONSERVATIVE Network. I couldn't believe he did it. I waited for the explosion from the members, I peeked over the edge of the parapit from my foxhole, I waited for the sound of protests from the conservatives to come firing back and put my hands over my ears, NOTHING HAPPENED. The responses Jud and I subsequently recieved were outstanding and I could not stop writing until it was finished the entire story . . . SO . . . . I had no chance to plan a story or plot. Here it is word for word what I typed daily as a series of 38 emails during the five week period. There is NO LESSON here and none intended . . . just a TRUE STORY about an ordinary warrior.

ENJOY a piece of my soul

Tommie Little

7th Dan
BushidoUSA.

Now you can hear from Jud.

I first met Tommie Little many years ago when I was managing the Spence for Governor Campaign in Sussex County Delaware during the early 2000's. When Terry dropped out in favor of John Burris, Tommie went back to Africa in total disgust with politics and I went to work for Burris. Regardless, Tommie and I e-mailed each other—back and forth—sharing ideas about politics and other philosophical aspects of our lives. We argued on email from 8000 miles real distance.

Tommie Little is defined as a former Marine Drill and Judo Instructor, lawyer, law professor, coach, international martial artist and former state legislator. He is a true character, tough as nails, brilliant, ingenious, creative and incredibly human. He also marches to a different drummer than most of us. Some people think he is nuts, I assure you, even his enemies know he is not, he is fiercely independent and hates the idea that others can influence or control his life. When he sent me his first email chapter of this story, I recognized that Tommie has something worthwhile to express and damn interesting to share. That's why I encouraged him to tell the whole story and have forwarded it to the Coastal Network which reaches close to 5000 folks daily. He sent me his entire story in over 3 dozen emails, which I in turn resent to my Network.

BY the way, Tommie Little's Nambian story is only the tip of the iceberg—there's plenty more in this fellow's life that is filled with adventure, intrigue, and learning that needs to be told. I'm happy to be involved in making it happen.

JUDSON Bennett-Coastal Network

Thank You

First, to my friend and inspiration for writing this accounting of my life in Africa, Judson Bennett, founder of the Coastal Conservative Network.

Second, to the Conservative Network itself for being so open minded and intelligent in continuing to encourage me to write.

Third, A SPECIAL OORAH to my Delaware First Responder Community, who ALWAYS inspire me to go beyond my own expectations of myself.

Fourth to all the personalities I named in this book . . . I loved you then and I love you now.

Last but not the least, MY EDITORS, Kristin Strouss-Peyton, Career Specialist and Rich Peyton, Program Manager of the Delaware Goodwill organization, great souls and good neighbors both, who voluntarily edited my awful prose so you can make sense out of my wanderings and adventures in Namibia.

I TRULY OWE YOU ALL A PERSONAL DEBT OF GRATITUDE . . . YOU ARE LIVING PROOF WARRIORS ARE OUT AND ABOUT . . . OORAH!

Chapter 1

It was a very HOT Monday in my small African village on the Caprivi Strip . . . 450 K from nowhere in Namibia, along the Zambesi River.

"Knock knock" . . . said Christoph, my 18 year old judo team leader . . . "Sensei time to go . . . .", my usual weekday after class routine . . . I napped every day after lunch of powdered instant soup and a tin of something or other in my mud hut. I got out from under my mosquito net and stretched . . . (it is always too hot to be outside in the heat of the afternoon so practice is at 4pm). I grabbed my two judo Gi's and opened the wooden door . . . Christoph and I held hands as we strolled out to the bush dojo through the searing hot sand (an African custom for men) and met my 12 member judo team practicing under shade trees in the sand. They were "moviezed" to believe Karate (a show off type punching and kicking) was the only martial arts in the world and never saw judo. It was time to introduce them to the real magic of self defense now that we began to trust each other.

I had been in the village a few very long hot weeks . . . today was the day. I threw my extra Gi to the first in line, a teen aged kid named Kennedy . . . he could literally jump OVER my head . . . quick wiry and strong, stood there transfixed . . . he put it on. I ordered "ATTACK" . . . he just stood there. African kids kneel before and are very submissive to their teachers . . . he was in shock. I yelled ATTACK . . . he did. I threw him hard into the sand and told the next in line to put the jacket on . . . this continued until I beat all 12 of them. I had to cheat and head butt the biggest one . . . . I was so completely exhausted, we laughed and laughed and celebrated our new warrior status as future Namibian Olympic judoka . . . it was the best day of my entire life . . . . I did it . . . I was thrilled I got an Olympic Judo team started in a third world country . . . . OORAH!

Christoph and I held hands as we strolled back to the village on a worn path through the bush together pulling on each other's hands the exact moment the other guys foot was ready to touch the sand and off balance each other . . . laughing, playing and trying to understand English and Maf'wue together.

I went into my hut took off the sandy jacket and pants, wrapped a large ki koi around me, grabbed my towel and strolled proudly through the village out to the hostile at Sikosinyana Senior Secondary School for a shower . . . the only one in many miles.

Only one knob necessary, no hot water, only smelly cold brown water from a bore hole deep in the ground . . . as the stream of cold water hit my head, I froze in place like a statue . . . SUDDENLY, I was shaking all over furiously . . . my hands could not grip the knob to turn it off . . . finally I struggled to the door and tried to hide the shakes . . . when I hit the sunshine they slowed down a bit but everyone in the village KNEW what was the matter with me, they would not look at me, it was impolite and I was an revered teacher and important American guest. I had contracted the dreaded malaria. Not just malaria, but cerebral malaria . . . the most dangerous African killer . . . once you succumb to the coma you never wake up. We all heard about it in training . . . we were all scared of it . . . I never took the damn pills . . . I knew they only delay the reaction after a mosquito bite causes it, a female don't cha know. I figured after a few bouts of it I would get immunized over time . . . WRONG!!!

The freezing shakes slowed down to a halt when I heated a bucket of water over a fire, poured it into a pan and stood in it. Then the fever and sweats hit . . . eeee gaddddddssss the fever and sweats were awful . . . I climbed out of the pan and made it to my rack (bed). I got under the mosquito net and laid on top of my sleeping bag . . . this routine lasted for days . . . in and out of searing hot delirium the freezing shakes and tremors were like being in an Antarctic earth quake . . . the fever and sweats like being in hell. I tried to teach . . . the principal asked me over and over what was wrong . . . I thought I had a case of bad flu . . . denial is a bitch . . . I would not admit I had the dreaded disease. I looked at the thermometer issued to me by the WorldTeach organization . . . the damn thing was in Celsius. 39.5 . . . hummmm didn't seem high to me??? (about 105 F or more, but what did I know)

Then the headache began . . . it was the worst most painful physical experience I ever had in my entire life. A softball size ball of searing migraine like pain rolling around in my head. With tears streaming down my face constantly, I begged God . . . PLEASSSSEEEE take me . . . I was afraid I would not die.

What a week it was . . . trying to fake it as a tough old American white man, in the remote African bush with malaria and no food: and complete my duties as a teacher of English classes at the same time; it was the worst act I ever put on. I was not kidding anyone, they could all plainly see what was happening to me . . . there is not a minute of privacy in a small village . . . everyone knows and hears everything in a tribal village . . . except for the conspiracy of silence about the dual lives lead by the male teachers with government bakki's. (Bakki's are pickup trucks). I found out about that much later.

***If you have a vehicle you can have a wife and life in the village and one in town, as well . . . so the guy teachers split on the weekends. It is really lonely on weekends in the village, the kids and women are wonderful, but very shy about talking to me.

The women helped me build a fire and heat water and the kids hovered about my hut listening to my only tape on my hand held recorder. If they asked in English I would play it again. I can still hear it . . . ABBA (when they made the movie Momma Mia . . . I nearly died laughing . . . I will never see it). I heard it hundreds of times, over and over, until I purposely ran out of batteries.

Chapter 2

Enough . . . Enough!

Finally sun fell I was alone in my hut, It was sweltering, no air moving that usually came in between the thatched roof and the mud wall, I had no food left and was drinking very little water, the beer drums had been going for hours. It was Saturday night . . . the Zambians across the river were getting drunk as lords from home made beer and beating them louder and louder . . . my head was splitting, I was sweating then shaking, sweating then shaking . . . I was heaving mightily every half hour (the dry kind) purple and yellow stuff came up once in a while . . . I knew I was in deep trouble and would not admit it. I begged for mercy . . . Please God, why had I been so bloody stupid and came to this God awful continent as a rookie in the first place . . . thinking I could handle it . . . .

YIKES!!! I went out into the bush in the dark . . . it was especially dark with no moon . . . hoping any animal would attack and kill me . . . I never felt so lonely, deserted and hopeless and desperate in my entire life.

I had walked to the regional government clinic the day before and I showed the thermometer to the Sangoma (witch doctor) on duty. They are actually great healers for those who they treat. He shrugged, he had no idea how to read it, I had showed it to all the women in the village, they knew nothing about it. He gave me aspirin . . . and said "push two now and two four times a day . . . sunrise, noon, sun fall, and before sleep". I started pushing them and felt worse. I was hallucinating every time I closed my eyes lying on my rack under the mosquito net. OH GOD please let me die . . . I pleaded!!!! I have no idea how many days passed like that . . . flashes of memory come as I write.

I remember the kids yelling and laughing, dogs barking, cattle braying . . . lion roaring, and hyena laughing out loud . . . then I lost it . . . I remember little after that . . . except bits and pieces like . . . the quiet after the generator at the school ran out of petrol . . . wishing I had a chair to sit on . . . and shade to sit under while outside during the day. There are too many mosquito's and humongous insects out at night but I figured "what the hell I had malaria anyway" was how I justified it as I sat on the cool sand in front of my hut staring at the Southern Cross sweeping across the night sky streaked with hot tears . . . the four stars represented me and my three kids . . . I thought of them every minute and I truthfully think that is why I finally made it . . . I was convinced they needed me to make it. I was determined to make it. I could not let this beat me . . .

Monday again . . . a whole week of this malaria crap . . . and I was beaten, depressed and begging for mercy . . . DAMN . . . I thought . . . "what a big sissy . . ."!!!

I'll forward Tommie's next transmission on his malaria experience, when it comes in. This guy is a something else!

Judson Bennett-Coastal Network

Chapter 3

I will not swear these next words are exactly accurate but pretty darn close . . . I did not have any idea what the exact weekdays were until much later when I listened to this part of my story over a year later. When I went to my duty station in the bush I carried a tape recorder to make a record of my exploits. I dictated every night on my trusty tape recorder . . . I kept a running journal. It was typed once I got back to America a year later and then printed in booklet form even later back in Namibia . . . I have one copy left. However, this writing is the true story, the other one I had typed has too much fluff and rhetoric in it, because I wanted to protect me and others from personal embarrassment. I haven't read the thing in many years, so here are the facts . . . fresh off the top of my head.

Monday morning my school principal ordered me to stop work immediately and take time to rest. I took the lead from the order to manage my escape from malaria land. I went to my hut and dug out a cardboard tube containing my lawyer graduation sheepskin from Delaware Law School . . . Juris Doctor. I out ranked him. I pointed, I'm a lawyer, a fact that was not to be known by a living soul IN NAMIBIA. I confronted him and said "I have rights, I am not a child, I want to work, etc" (actually in my defense I was totally delirious, yet somehow knew the act I was putting on was my ticket out of the village). He immediately ordered me to town to go to a hospital. It worked . . . but, talk about shame . . . I was burning with shame . . . I knew I was officially a quitter . . . and everyone at home in America would know it. I slinked to my hut and crawled into my sleeping bag. The hallucinations were fantastic, I kept seeing my Uncle Connie, I had helped him die a few years before . . . he pestered me and pestered me to stay awake. I saw many others who were still alive in America and one in particular was a young girl named Julie, another World Teacher stationed about 50 k away. She had her hands on her hips castigating me constantly for not taking the malaria pills. I can still see her today as I type. I have no idea what happened for the next two days . . . but no one would come near me in the village.

Wednesday afternoon all the male teachers in the village were going away for a long Easter weekend, everyone was excited, I was totally whipped. My hut neighbor was off to town and said he had room for me . . . I really struggled to keep up a good front . . . they could see the suffering on my face and I lost so much weight my pants kept falling off. I sat shot gun so the air would cool me down . . . in and out of consciousness . . . hours later we arrived at a house I gave directions to in the tiny one phone town of Katima Mulilo. Henry the Roonik . . . (Afrikaner for the redneck BRIT) . . . these two species hated each other. Henry blurted, as I walked up his driveway, "Oh my God it's good to see you mate . . . your dying." "Naaaaa just a bad cold, Henry, I'll be alright in your air conditioned living room". "Like hell, you're going straight to the hospital you have malaria". Off we went in his bakki and damn if we didn't meet Issac the local Sangoma an old friend of mine, waiting for me like he was expecting me, how could he have known, there were no phones, it was late and almost dark . . . whew . . . he gave me QUININE ASAP . . . then a large bag of quinine pills to take home to Henry's for the night.

On the way back my headache eased, Henry announced, he and his lovely French wife are going on holiday for ten days: would I live at the house until they return??? Robbery is the local industry in Caprivi and God help the dope that leaves his home unprotected . . . "it's a bloody miracle . . .", I yelled joyfully, "ten days in an air conditioned bed room and after a good SLEEP then maybe food". "It's a bloody fookin miracle", yelled my savior "Henry the Roonik". You Americans are all crazy you know that . . ."

I went straight to bed, they were gone when I awoke, I was drenched in sweat . . . the sheets, the mattress . . . pools of water on the floor beside me. I was so weak I could barely stand. I stripped the bed, propped the mattress on its side to dry and went into the bathroom and threw the sheets and blanket into the tub. I knelt down to stir them. As the smelly cold brown water ran into the tub, the smell of the water made me nauseous, and I started heaving again then passed out. I awoke as the tub was running over and turned off the tap, passed out again and that is the last I remember for a long while. The next thing I heard was a voice yelling "Father Judo, Father Judo". It was Michele, an Egyptian Judo player also stationed in Caprivi at a vocational school, how he possibly could have known I was at Henry's is still a mystery to me. HE SAVED MY LIFE!

I'm really getting into this story . . . I think its therapy time . . . I should do this writing and it should be read, so thanks for reading!

Chapter 4

The News Journal headline could easily have been . . . "MUSLIMS SAVE CHRISTIAN . . . lawyer saved on Holy Thursday!"

I could not speak, but I knew it was Michele carrying me, Oh my dearest Michele, an Arab with great English . . . my first glimpse of him was many months ago as he did a surprise rolling judo break-fall from the dining room of the Guinea Fowl Inn slamming the wooden floor like a crack of thunder on the porch where I was sitting quietly alone sipping my afternoon tea. CRASH! He jumped up, saluted judo style (a deep bow) and grinned from ear to ear . . . "Welcome Father Judo . . . how can Egypt be of service" . . . a typical judo reaction from a lower to higher belt all over the world. We hugged, wrestled a bit and established superiority, again a common custom in International Judo. Two beautiful young local girls appeared from the shadow behind him . . . "Meet my students".

I had no idea how locals always knew exactly where I was . . . . A few weeks before, I started an exercise class on the slooping back lawn of the Inn right next to the Zambesi River . . . one guy was always assigned to watch for the crocs and I would teach break falls to the others. Two postman were dragged off the banks during the past week and the entire population was on alert for them. The break-fall is a critical Judo protective move that is critical to learning self defense of any kind; but rarely taught except in Olympic judo. It assures no injuries when being thrown hard in practice sessions and tournaments. It is the entire reason Judo is not a popular sport in America . . . it is to threatening physically and learning Karate is just taking a punch or kick once in a while . . . WE THROW HARD, every single time, you must learn the break-fall first!

The government was trying to sort out where my village teaching station was located. I was stuck in Katima Mulilo at the only Inn and was the only guest for two months. Except for week day over night foreign travelers from all types of English speaking countries. Namibia just became independent and English was mandated in the constitution. We English speaking peoples were in a race to take over their culture . . . it was outright embarrassing. I hated that part! However, I was stuck at the Inn. I heard tremendous stories from every part of our world on the porch at night after dinner. I was slapping mosquitos together with the machos while they put away gallons of beer and gin, until it got too much, even for the old salts in Africa. I was out of money anyway and waiting patiently every day to hear from the government when and where I was going and anxious to see my mud hut. Michele made up for any personal inconvenience, real or imagined . . . I loved the guy.

He and the ladies came to join my first Namibia Judo group . . . I was thrilled the word was out that a Master Judo teacher from America was around. I will now admit, I could have cared less about high school teaching, judo was my only hidden agenda for the whole idea of going to a third world country in the first place. I kept it entirely secret from the WorldTeach organization but had told my friend Joe Biden of my intention before I left America and on arrival the Namibian Ambassador called me to his private office and after a very stern lecture about not interfering into Namibian affairs, smiled broadly, wished me well and gave me permission privately to pursue Olympic Judo ON MY OWN. I would receive absolutely NO support whatsoever. I smiled, "Thank you SIR! . . . saluting with clicking flip-flops . . . and I could have kissed Joe". The ONLY condition was, I had to do it entirely by word of mouth and accept all comers, first come first serve, and could not favor any language or special interests.

I teared up when Michele bowed as first leader of the first official Namibian Olympic Judo group. And . . . we soon had a small group of Namibians practicing break-falls on the hard nubby sand every day . . . taking turns on the croc watch . . . as I yelled . . . Hajime! I told Michele what to say in English and he in turn told them what he thought I meant in local language, he told them when they complained about the sting of the slap on hard sand, "Under Tommie Sensei, we were so fortunate, the rest of world judo are sissy's . . . they use mats."

He screamed when he saw me . . . "Tommie Sensei, you're dying, I will be right back" . . . hopped on his bicycle and spun wheels . . . I do not know what happened next because I woke up in the hospital Good Friday afternoon tubes coming out of everywhere and people looking down at me shaking their heads in that African way. I had no idea, I had been carried, thought of as dead, by two Egyptian MUSLIMS on the Christian Holy Thursday . . . God certainly loves the multitude! I felt terrific . . . I kept telling them I was OK. They paid absolutely NO ATTENTION. I yelled at the top of my voice . . . they couldn't hear or understand me, I didn't know which . . . all of a sudden I was looking at me lying on a cot with tubes sticking in me and the top of the shaking heads . . . I tried to say . . . I felt fantastic!!!

I drifted pleasantly, off somewhere, and saw Uncle Connie again; he was holding the light ball he kept bouncing off my chest when I was falling asleep in my hut all through the past week. His voice was a beckoning, an understanding, not words. He had a beautiful white silkish outfit on looking 20 ish . . . I answered "where the hell am I", He beckoned to me . . .

I am ONE

You are ONE

We are each other

Oneness is our Mother/Father

There is no other.

As he beckoned those words I immediately understood exactly where I was and where I fit. I was safe and sound and FINALLY at HOME!

This writing exercise is doing me a real personal service remembering this stuff. I had never talked about my real role in Namibia before. Thanks Jud Bennett for your motivation, you are a first class friend and warrior.

Chapter 5

NOTE***

SO as not to add any unconscious suggestion to your current point of view or add any new view to the events in this material, I am giving you my exact words that were lifted from the tape that I carried with me for years . . . I dictated it right after I returned to Henry's house after the hospital . . . so although it may sound a bit constrained OR THOUGHT UP . . . REMEMBER I WAS SUMMARIZING MY IMMEDIATE IMPRESSIONS because I did not want to lose the essence of the reality of my personal experience . . . I remembered many other details LATER as I got more distant and healed from the events . . . so here it is dudes fresh from the other side, the very day I awoke . . .

"After a while of watching someone fooling with my arms and wondering just what the excitement was all about . . . I felt terrific . . . I sensed I was out of my body staring down at it . . . I floated off . . . alone. This is what I sensed most."

"ONENESS . . . a knowing feeling of understanding, of protection and of observation, IT IS an OVERPOWERING feeling of security, of being held safe and sound in the arms of something invisible. IT is like the runners high, a feeling of being alive after a great workout. a hot shower, massage, then finishing a long overdue tasty meal . . . everything is alright and is always going to be in your favor . . . . there is no sense of threat or loss whatsoever . . . no sense of a place to go and all the time necessary to get there . . ."

"ONENESS is SO DAMN OBVIOUS it is amusing when you understand it . . . I burst out laughing . . . I wondered WHY I had I never felt it before, it's so simple and makes so much sense. Oneness includes the smallest quark and the space between every atom in all material that exists. The UNIVERSE is ONE big interconnected energy vibration, an actual living vibrating organism . . . it blew my mind and also blew away all my former thoughts of spiritual concepts . . . . ONENESS . . . . that's it . . . that is the whole deal . . . . ONENESS . . . . no more . . . no less . . . we are ONENESS."

"I cannot explain it any other way. It is not a person, philosophy, idea, dogma, concept, belief or thing . . . it is just there . . . I sensed everything else is totally subordinate to it, part of it and dependent upon it . . . . many have a notion that GOD, ALLAH, RA, TAO, JEHOVAH. YAHWEH, the GREAT SPIRIT, THE UNIVERSE, WHATEVER is made like us . . . . WRONG!!!!! . . . we are all ONENESS . . . . any other concept of any deity being separate or different from ONENESS is DENIAL!!!!!" (Sort of like a fish denying water exists . . . or a bird . . . air)

"As soon as I realized I was no longer in my body, which looked silly as hell lying there anyway, I felt really embarrassed because I sensed this ONENESS surrounding and completely enveloping me and I realized how wrong I was about GOD all these years. I thought others that I sensed near me could see how stupid I was. I had suddenly realized ONENESS . . . it scared the hell out of me, then all of a sudden, I felt fantastic . . . incredible . . . I felt accepted as part of a family. I had no sense of stress or personal guilt or limitation, the sense of PEACE and being HAPPY was overwhelming . . . I lost all fear of absolutely everything and anything . . . . then the visitors (teachers) came . . ."

I had a million questions ready . . . but first, I beckoned to Uncle Connie with a big grin, "what came first . . . the chicken or the egg", We laughed EXPLOSIVELY for what seemed an eternity until all the stress of my illness and emotional trauma accumulated from my recent sickness and dibilitating earth visit was gone . . . "You tell me," he smiled . . . I REALLY LOVE THAT MAN!

I will now relate recollections about how I awoke EASTER MORNING!

I figured out, why Uncle Connie was bouncing the ball of pure light off my chest for the week before the trip to the hospital . . . he was keeping me AWAKE in my body . . . everyone in Caprivi knew that if you have cerebral malaria and fall into a coma you will never wake up. The doctors wife died the day before I arrived at the hospital, he could not save her and there were 302 victims in this particular epidemic of cerebral malaria during this period of a few weeks in Caprivi . . . all died but one . . . . that would be me!

Someday I will write my insights gained on the other side . . . but for now leave it with this promise . . . if I could get back there again, right now, no matter what I was offered to stay here, I will leave this very instant. There is NOTHING to fear in death, it is not real, it is only a simple change from this life dimension through a door to our HOME dimension with our real family in this UNIVERSE of ONENESS . . . enough said OK.

During the Good Friday, Holy Saturday, delicious sojourn to the other side, I stopped back often to the hospital room and watched people working on my body . . . then off I'd go again with Uncle Connie, he was always smiling like a proud Father, he acted as my guide to everything I wanted to see or know. He beckoned, "Tommie you will not stay here, this is an introductory visit you will return." N o matter how much I begged and pleaded, he insisted I would return to my body. That sucked! I did not want to return and persisted in arguing my case to the teachers with a pissed off grin.

Suddenly, I sat up and grabbed a priest's cassock at the waist. I scared the hell out of him. He was in the middle of the LAST RITES, candles burning, in the down stroke of the catholic blessing after anointing my cold head. Everyone ran out of the room. I was crying loudly begging for help . . . until this very moment I never admitted why . . . I wanted to GO BACK HOME with Uncle Connie. I was totally pissed off to be back in this tired old body.

I refused any further treatment, pulled the needles and tubes out, left the hospital totally pissed off and walked a few K in the heat through the sand to Henry's house. The back door was still open, nothing was stolen. I grabbed my recorder and after calming down from crying and moaning . . . dictated as much as I could remember of this death experience. I will organize my thoughts, I am being motivated to continue with my African story and after a bit will continue to write the rest of my Namibian experience . . . thanks for reading my friend . . . YOU MADE ME feel good that I am alive to tell you this tale . . . YOU remind me of WHO I AM!

As a footnote . . . I can tell you only this fact that was embedded within me, as a result of my visit to the other side, I know for certain our greatest spiritual challenge in our present time is . . .

LOVE YOUR NEIGHBOR . . . and . . . THERE ARE NO EXCEPTIONS!

Hey everyone . . . Happy Fathers Day . . . When I see my kids with my grand children I am truly happy to be alive . . . . OORAH!!!

Chapter 6

Damn . . . if I ever wanted to drink . . . this was my chance to do it error free and NEVER get caught . . . (that's how alcoholics think). I was feeling much better . . . and . . . taking all the credit as usual . . . there was plenty of booze in the dining room and closets. Henry and his Lady (I can't remember her name) are not due back from Hentis Baii for a few days yet . . . I am totally alone . . . fresh off near death, in a feerrred O nuttin, kind of pissed off mood. I am sober from the devils favorite brew; that's a stupid joke there is NO DEVIL . . . how could there be in a ONENESS. I'm in a grateful mood and worked from 8 this morning in court to 9 tonight teaching at a university . . . I am turned on by you the reader as a real live audience and your response letters about similar experiences blow my mind . . . so the hell with it . . . here's more.

On the 26th of June 29 years ago . . . it all started that day with two other guys (one is reading this letter and will send it to the other) "wanna meet a new politician" . . . "Yeah" . . . I would use any excuse to quit work practicing law in my Trolley Square office and go to the Del Rose Cafe. I was in a "Drafts for everyone and bring me yer best bar maid" kind of mood . . . ya know what I mean dudes. I was ready for the fun to start any minute now right after I down this beer. 4 pm . . . "I gaattt ta ga oooome" I says intelligently to the fine gentlemen at the bar and off I staggered to my car . . . acting sober as a judge for the casual observers in the Del Rose . . . that is until the warm air outside hit my face . . .

My wife always knew. So did my kids . . . a drinking problem in anyone is always an obvious thing. Notice how drunks get pissed off when you tell them they have a drinking problem . . . it's called DENIAL Well I was the original "EGYPTIAN from the land of DENIAL".I always knew about my own drunken father who died in a Salvation Army for the homeless . . . I was abandoned for a couple bottles of beer as a youngin . . . but I did not mind that a damn bit to tell the honest truth. I'll be darned . . . damn that felt good. I always pretended to love and respect my father . . . (small letter intentional) but then I was always defending him ya see . . . I was always totally disappointed and embarrassed by and for him and for my little brother . . . I learned manipulation as my way out . . . my brother learned rebelliousness . . . he died a very lonely man a few years ago while I was in Africa . . . . anyway

I staggered up to our third floor bedroom and plopped to sleep . . . woke up after 6 still drunk, bathed . . . shaved and went out on some phony pretense or other . . . everyone KNEW . . . I knew they KNEW . . . it was awful. I went to George's next Door a favorite hangout for other drunks . . . I finished the job . . . by 9 I did a flying one and a half off the back of the bar stool while tilting a Jameson's'"neat . . . . I was knocked OUT COLD!

I DROVE myself home after fighting a friend for my car keys . . . I crawled up three flights . . . fell on the floor pants down in the bathroom stuff coming out both ends . . . I heard a voice . . . "DAD!!!" It was my oldest daughter and it scared the shit out of me . . . I haven't touched a drink since . . . OORAH ANNIE!

Chapter 7

Henry and his Lovely Lady came back from the coast one fine sunny day. I walked out into the back yard as I heard them drive up in their 4 wheeler SUV; I wanted to help them unload. She gasped . . . "Oh my God Tommie, you look like you were in a concentration camp." I was at my all time low in body weight and general health; I had no mirror in the bush, so I knew nothing about my looks for many months. It was liberating and I absentmindedly grew to not miss the MIRROR, MIRROR on the wall. She demanded, "Go into our bedroom drop your pants and take a good look in the mirror" I obeyed. "Oh my God", I gasped. I did look like I was truly a starving old man, bones sticking out all over . . . no butt . . . no chest . . . bony ribs, knobby knees, just pure skin and bones. I finally broke down completely, I could not stop crying, it was a massive pity party. WHY had I been so bloody stupid to think I could handle the African bush at my age . . . damn, I was the dumbest man on the face of the earth. I ruined my body, my mind, and was left with only a whimsical spiritual reality that NO ONE will ever believe in a million years YEEEE GADS!

Gruff old Henry turned into an immediate Sgt Major . . . "OK boy your gonna eat" . . . they fed me 6 times a day, nothing would stay down, they woke me up for food, I drank gallons of fresh milk and ate bread and jelly. Finally I got hungry for real food and put in a few good night's sleep. After two weeks, "I'm OK", I announced!

Henry knew I needed to head for civilization at the Namibian capital of Windhoek, he knew I should report to the catholic mission, /I /Gams, (slashes / are pronounced as clicks) where I trained with the others in WorldTeach before I was assigned my bush duty station. He said he would pick up my sea bags and stuff at the village and I insisted on going with him, although I hated the very thought of that trip. They all cheered when they saw me, they heard about me waking up in the hospital and wanted to touch me. I was very embarrassed, They called me a new name that I did not understand, I had to leave, quickly, I could not get my eyes to stop crying. We left the village; it was the saddest day of my entire life. "Henry what does Madala mean". "It means . . . the wise old man who knows everything". Two days later, Madala was off to Windhoek. What a trip.

My lovely French lady packed me a dozen peanut butter and jelly sandwiches . . . and I had my trusty canteen full of smelly water. Henry told the cops who I was and they were only too glad to take me along on an official (in uniform) trip . . . three of them and me. Only three of us could fit in the bakki cab with one cop always taking turns crouching behind the cab in the wind swept back of the open bakki. We were speeding over the dusty gravel road looking for elephant heading toward civilization 450 k away, chatting in English and telling stories to each other, suddenly, after many, many hot sweaty hours we saw a stranded prison bus on the side of the road in front of us, we slowed cautiously and stopped. They drew their AK 47's and signaled to the group of stranded prisoners and their supervisors to identify themselves, after the formalities, introductions and an emergency radio call for help. I was told, they had been there two days. They ran out of food and water yesterday; we edged the bakki up to the bus, I was ordered to stay put. The prisoners looked whipped, forlorn and sad. One in particular lifted his eyes, glanced at me, and I jumped out of the bakki and gave them each a half sandwich and a large gulp of my smelly water . . . the cops were quiet so not to embarrass me in front of them, but stared me down, until I gave it all away.

When the dust settled, we hopped back into the bakki and we left, confident the government would send a replacement bus with food and water. After a while, the driver pulled to the roadside under a rare tall shade tree, we stretched under the tree listening for wildlife. I saw them laying out their food carefully on the hood. They were laughing and pointing at me for having nothing to eat; I sat under the tree and said nothing. The head cop said in English "Did you learn anything American?" I said sarcastically, "Like what?". He laughed with the others, "you gave away your food and water, now you will starve to death if we break down," they howled, and teased me, eating and chewing with exaggerated slowness, until I smiled, then offered me a half sandwich and a swig from a plastic bottle. I gave them my beautiful empty canteen for another half and another swig of the tasty brown smelly water. They laughed all the way to Windhoek at the stupidity of Americans. Frankly, I smiled all the way, I knew what I was doing and would never change, I was a United States Marine.

At /I /Gams front gate, 3 am . . . the police bakki pulled up . . . the Dutch Brother Superior in his nightie swung the heavy gate open . . . peered into the dark, "Tommie, we heard you died" "I did . . . it was great", I said with phony bravado, smiling broadly, the cops carrying my bags . . . once my feet crossed the line into the mission I collapsed in his arms!

Man, I'm hungry . . . I think I will go get a cheese burger, then try to remember the rest of my arrival story at /I /Gams a Roman Catholic Dutch Missionary Brotherhood in Windhoek.

I awoke the next day at the sound of a rooster crowing at the first sniff of daylight, right in my ear next to the window like it had all through WorldTeach training. I shared this room with Jimmy a 22 year old kid from Chicago . . . my very best friend and roommate. He had beautiful straight black hair all the way down to his waist that girls would kill for, there was nothing feminine about Jimmy he was straight as an arrow, our personal sexual preference was the first thing we spoke about. We knew upon eye contact in the New York airport we were destined to be friends and hung out together and roomed together through the whole trip and in training . . . a very funny dude, my friend Jimmy. But where was he, where was I, it seemed like a dream or deja vu all over again to steal a phrase. “Knock knock”, did I want to attend mass . . . “you bet your sweet boppie”, I yelled. And Brother and I went to the mission house to pray together at mass, I was invited to breakfast. Mass was incredible fun, It was the first time in my whole life I knew actually who and what I was talking to . . . it felt great . . . I haven’t stopped talking to “it” since.

AT BREAKFAST AFTER EATING, CONVERSATION TURNED TO MY EXPERIENCE, I WAS SHY ABOUT CLAIMING ANYTHING in front of such gentle and beautiful religious men. BUT THEY PRESSED AND QUESTIONED! So I unloaded . . . they loved it, said I should write as much as I can remember at the mission while healing. Brother helped me back to my room and I plopped on to my rack, exhausted and ready for the humiliating trip back to the States. Before I left America, Ted Caddell, the reporter from the News Journal

Papers took bets on how long I would last in the bush . . . . YIKES . . . I was a total failure. Thrown out of my job for getting sick, a sissy, what would Marines think of me now? I fell asleep fast because I knew I was safe.

Two weeks of walking down and up the steep winding hills in Windhoek to get a tea and biscuit every day forced me to exercise and built my legs and my wind. Brother took me to the local Afrikaner Doctor, After a through exam, he enthusiastically pronounced me fit . . . then seriously "You have an angel following you mate, you truly should not be alive" I said "I have more than one", winked and we both laughed as he gave me wellness instructions on how to get fit and well again. Two weeks of talking to Brother about my trip to the other side and hearing his own other side experience kept me sane. However, as hard as I rationalized my experience I failed my mission and I could not face going home to America. Jane my next door neighbor in Wilmington found me and called . . . I was broke and asked her to send me some money I had given her before I left the states anticipating an emergency just like this . . . "call John Flaherty at Biden's office and see what can be done to get some cash over here, I'm flat broke"

I met a lady named Erna at a dinner party with British diamond sorters . . . (that's another story), she was my Afrikaner teacher in training and I heard her say she would love to drive to the west coast through the Namib desert to Swakopmund . . . I asked her if I could hitch a ride. Her boyfriend was gay and announced he could have cared less if we went on a trip together. This attitude of openness and tolerance was new for me to witness . . . amazing. And . . . she loaned me money until I got some cash to pay her back . . . a great soul, a real friend. We talked about the history of Namibia from the Afrikaner point of view . . . I had never heard it before . . . aparthide (legal separation of the races) made sense to them. We drove all day to Swakopmund, had a great lunch on the strand among the tall beautiful palm trees at the Strand Hotel. I marveled at the convenience stores and friendliness of this small German built town in Africa, nothing I had seen to date was as beautiful as Swakopmund . . . I fell in love at first sight . . . we traveled on up the Namib desert coast along the lonely and cold Atlantic Ocean, past the salt farms staring at the waves crashing to Henry's cottage right on the beach at Hentis Baii. He encouraged me to visit it and called the security team in advance while I was at his house in

Caprivi, they were waiting for our arrival. We spent a platonic weekend walking and talking about the South African political situation and she educated me about the other side . . . hers.

Well although I did not touch booze in Caprivi I did bring a simple truth back from the other side . . . I know I am truly an alcoholic—truly . . . I swear to that . . .

Chapter 8

I AM BEING PUSHED TO WRITE THIS STORY... BUT YOU ALREADY KNOW THAT . . . I am not particularly fond of writing this embarrassing material . . . I am real good at keeping secrets . . . but, I get to read the story as I type it and IT IS FRESH FROM A CLEAR MEMORY . . . NO NOTES . . . I sit to type. Then see it happening in my mind, I type it as I see it happening and as I see my audience SEEING it . . . I am frequently amused and totally embarrassed . . . SO . . .

OVERCOMING MY FEAR OF STARTING OVER has always been my personal demon . . . spawned by my FEAR of ABANDONMENT.

By Sunday afternoon I felt almost human again, I felt strong, but sensed a familiar FEAR approaching. I asked Erna to leave me in Swakopmund with my sleepy bag and dob kit. I had heard strong rumors at the mission that Jimmy was somewhere on the coast and I was hell bent to find him. I was relaxed after a few days of Erna's history lessons and long walks in the sand, soothed by small freezing waves crashing over my ankles and calf's. I tanned slowly and lost my sense of FEAR of white Afrikaners. I looked into a mirror the last day and actually looked healthy and happy. I was on a real high for weeks, it frightened me . . . it felt like I was on some kind of magic drug. I felt invincible and strong as an OX . . . BUT . . . MOST IMPORTANTLY . . . Somehow; I knew for certain I had to face my FEARS again. I had an incredible urge that I must make friends with my fears, fear of rejection, fear of abandonment, fear of failure, fear of dying, fear of starving, fear of loneliness, fear of mosquito's. fear of just about everything and anything that moves in either America or Africa. I had NOTHING LEFT BUT FEAR, I had NO personal possessions in an unfamiliar foreign country, NO language, NO VISA, NO sponsor, NO job, NO money, NO clothing, NOTHING to eat or drink, NO place to lay my head, NO friends, NO family or relatives . . . I ended up just like my OLD MAN . . . COMPLETELY HOMELESS, full of FEAR . . . and . . . looking for handouts from strangers in the streets!

After a fierce argument, Erna dropped me off reluctantly at the Mole, an Atlantic Ocean cove and gorgeous beach behind a great stone jetty shaped like a half moon around it, otherwise 8000 miles of ocean was in front of me looking straight at Wilmington Delaware. I walked slowly around the area, then tentatively toward the empty beach observing everything in sight or hearing, as I was trained to do, hummmmmm . . . well kept, no trash and the sand raked. I sat down carefully in the sand glancing around and seeing no witnesses I HAD A GOOD OLD FASHIONED SHOULDER SHAKING GUT WRENCHING CRY. I knew for sure I was done for, I was beaten, There was absolutely no hope for recovery, I was alone and finally out for the count. I tilted my face toward the brilliant sun and screamed as loud as I could, in total and absolute frustration, defeat and desperation . . . "OK OK OK OOOO KKKK . . . . I GIVE UP . . . YOU WIN . . . I GIVE UP".

INSTANTLY: A loud voice appeared in my head, "GIVE UP WHAT. TOMMIE, GIVE UP WHAT!"

Suddenly, I laughed myself silly, I rolled over in the sand . . . I GOT IT . . . I realized I got exactly what I always wanted . . . a chance to start the race over from a complete dead STOP. I had begged since the late 70's for a brand new start, begged, pleaded, BEGGED! My exaggerated laughter slowed down to a smile, it was like being shot between the eyes with a silver bullet . . . I understood the exact point of the message I HAD NOTHING LEFT TO GIVE UP . . . . and got up. Without any hesitation whatsoever, I walked what seemed a few blocks to the nearest residential homes and started knocking on doors. "I'm an American, does anyone speak English", yelling loudly, pointing at my mouth. At the 6th house, a little kid took my hand and lead me several blocks away, knocked on a door, stepped back politely, so the answering person would see me first and waited . . . the door opened slowly . . . The familiar face appeared, JIMMY in total shock, yelled, racing to hug me . . . "Tommie, we heard you died . . ." . . . and almost bowled me over, "I did . . . it was great" and we laughed till we cried. I profusely thanked the kid and the kid went away laughing at us laughing. GOD we laughed hard, "I made it! I fookin MADE IT!" I screamed over and over, beating my chest, imitating my newly found Afrikaner cultural personality.

He pushed me through the door, threw my bag and kit into a corner. I asked Jimmy if I could sit in the only chair sitting in the center of the room, "I need to chill out a bit and relax" . . . "hell", he said, "I can do better than that my brother" and with a big old fashioned grinning American Indian ceremonial flair, reached for something in an ash tray on the floor and ceremoniously and conspiratorially lit up a humongous joint. When he got it fired to his satisfaction he began circling me continuously like an Native American shaman at a tribal war dance . . . continually blowing smoke directly at my face, I would never admit to inhaling, but something changed, I felt my shoulders involuntarily sag, my tension letting go and my knots in my solar plex relaxing. After a few moments, I couldn't talk, but smiled at his antics, as red hot steamy tears streamed truthfully down my face, I WAS LOST and MY BROTHER JIMMY FOUND ME!

An hour later, we were both laughing out loud about our mutually miserable African experiences, we decided "Screw WorldTeach . . . let's switch jobs". He wanted to go to the bush and die for his country like I did, I wanted to teach English in civilization, where I was certain I would find some kind of mats. It made sense to both of us and seemed like a fair trade. Now, all we had to do is convince The Rossing Foundation to hire me, convince the he US Government to approve my VISA, convince WorldTeach to approve a transfer to Jimmy's new duty station . . . there were plenty of openings members dropped out frequently and another of our team recently died of menengitus, she was a great gal with a hugh sense of humor, and most important I liked her. Finally we had to convince the Republic of Namibia to approve of the whole idea, and then find enough money to survive till we got done.

The plot thickens:

Den Den Den DENNNNNN . . . Enter stage right:

John Flaherty from Senator Joe Biden's Office . . . OORAH . . . . and . . . . I MEAN . . . OOOOOOOOOOOOOOOORAH!!!!! A STANDING OVATION FOR THE CALVERY!

Next day, I got a surprise phone call from my friend Jane in Wilmington . . . how she found me at The Rossing Foundation school, was beyond my imagination . . . "John said Joe Biden will get your money to you somehow." (Truly,

I could kiss that man). I convinced Ursala, Jimmy's boss at Rossing, that I could easily take over his English classes at the foundation school in Venita, a suburb of Swakopmund, yet within city limits, Most of you would immediately recognize the contrast of separation of classes (no whites) . . . just me! Jimmy choose to live in town and he would soon go off to the bush . . . the added incentive to all parties for the whole deal was, "Ursala I can also teach Criminal Law in English to the police!" Waving my Delaware Law School diploma at her, she absolutely loved that idea and got solidly behind the formalities of the switch. She was so sure we could pull it off, I was given a bed to sleep in, a roof over my head, a few bucks in advance . . . and a promise of dinner at her house with her husband and family a few nights a week until I could afford to pay to eat. Through her alone, by the end of the meeting, I felt a family connection to the Swakopmund community . . . . and boy was I psyched at her interest in me starting my Olympic Development National Judo team starting with the COPS! I was back in the game . . . . OORAH!

HINT:

*** Please note . . . . THIS ENTIRE RECOVERY WAS COMPLETED WITHIN 24 HOURS OF MY DESPERATE PRAYER ON THE BEACH!

Chapter 9

I had no idea I was the answer to Jimmy's prayers. It was no secret he was long disgusted at the Rossing job, teaching 5 uranium workers English every night and filling the day with "make up work"; we were asked to justify our positions with BS type grade school hang it on the fridge stuff . . . hell the most important day of the week was the Friday Noon tea party required to be attended by all Rossing staff, both foreign and domestic. At first I thought everyone looked cute in local costume and that it served a legitimate bonding purpose, as was the officially touted head lady's reasoning . . . . then I soon realized they were mind deadening boring gossip sessions with the queen bee . . . if it wasn't for the free food I would have found my own way out.

Jimmy had ambition as a photographer and really wanted his "out in the bush" American volunteer action . . . he already had a somewhat rowdy social reputation in town, especially with photographing of ladies. He was my buddy, but we never socialized together . . . age is a funny factor; I have the wish to do young things . . . but not the energy. I was really into recording my Caprivi story to tell someday and stayed home, while Dione, my other roommate (a volunteer Australian lady) and Jimmy caroused in town after dark. Dione with her future husband and Jimmy with . . . who knows! One night he insisted I meet him at Swakop's only after hours club to play pool. KELLY'S was situated on the main drag in the center of town . . . when a town has only 8 square blocks, surrounded by residential suburbs and worker townships, then desert dunes for miles and miles, center is easy to find. I found it.

"Jimmy what the . . . this is a gay bar", I whispered quietly, after he introduced me to the owner, an openly gay British guy in a country where it is SERIOUSLY ILLEGAL to be gay. I wandered over to buy a coke at the bar and the owner slip-slided up to me and offered to pay for my drink. I knew he was hitting on me and that he was prepared to give me the old come on, "everyone is a bit gay" sales pitch. I let him go for it, for about ten minutes, as I sipped my coke and absentmindedly gazed around at the writhing bodies on the dance floor, especially one couple in particular: then, when he thought I had finally bought into his point of view and let my guard down, he stopped selling. I jumped in quickly and said "YOUR DEAD WRONG DUDE, look out at the dance floor and try to guess which couple I've been looking at??". It was full of men dancing with men, women dancing with women, men and women dancing alone and together in a very sexy Latin type slow dance. A very handsome well stacked mannish lesbian Afrikaner was making out with a very beautiful, well built very sexy German lesbian, both leaning against the wall on the crowded dance floor and really going at it . . . he pointed to one couple after another and guessed four or five more times . . . he never got it right . . . I was watching the sexy lesbians, I couldn't take my eyes off them, they were the sexiest turn on I ever witnessed . . . and it made my point to the owner. He left me be . . . later, we actually became friends!

Jimmy left . . . I inherited his metal frame bed in Dione's room. I was sleeping on the floor with the chair . . . now I had a metal frame with bare springs, but NO mattress, and my trusty sleepy bag, bought for me by the Delaware Prosecutors I served with as a Public Defender in Family Court and presented by Adam Balick, along with other things for use in Africa before I shipped out. I settled down and got back into good physical shape by a routine of 7 miles a day walking to and from the foundation school . . . eating regularly, sleeping regularly, walking around to the shops in town, thinking about "How do I get Judo going" . . . suddenly, I bumped face to face into a full bearded Afrikaans speaking German Doctor, the father of Dione's beau. "Hey, mate, do you need a SEMPEI? (a Japanese word title meaning OLDER MAN AS MENTOR) I sensed he was serious and understood my adopted Japanese warrior culture of mental discipline, we talked, he really did understand the warrior culture; he had been a top medical officer in the South African army and I needed him. I accepted, my life took on another positive turn and he remains one of my very best friends today. He receives all my emails (including this accounting) and has ever since I returned to the States 4 years ago . . . OORAH!!!! His name is Wotan, but I call him Dr. Wonderful . . . maybe he will visit us someday!

Wotan said "I hear there are gymnastic mats on the floor of a big room not used in the evenings at the English High School in Venita",

"I live close to there", I said . . . and that was the beginning of a beautiful friendship!!!

A week or so later . . .

The three day CSI police class/seminar/workshop sessions . . . whatever you call these things, were set up by Ursala and the Swakop head cop "Hennie". It was a Rossing Foundation NGO experiment to specifically train the entire west coast region of Namibia; Swakopmund, Arandis, Walvis and Hentis Baii police in the Constitutionally mandated ENGLISH language to help them recognize and protect the validity of possible valuable forensic evidence on the scene of a suspected crime for testimony in trials. If it worked it could easily go national and Rossing was a powerfully politically connected organization through their Uranium Mining interests. I was a Public Defender for 11 years in Delaware criminal courts with oodles of experience in criminal trials, so, I became the perfect person to set up and lead criminal evidence investigation drills for cops . . . what a blast . . .

finally, I was doing something that will benefit this new English speaking democratic nation.

Some cops . . . had . . . some English, but all cops had Afrikaans, the language they learned as children in the schools and hostels of the old South African apartheid regimes where English was forbidden. Namibia was called South West Africa before independence. During our 22 hour crossing of the Atlantic from New York to South Africa I met and spoke at length with Nelson Mandala, a true hero to blacks, colored and whites alike in these parts. I asked bluntly what I should teach. He explained the best value I could leave behind from my personal volunteer effort in Africa was to teach racial tolerance and "Love your Neighbor" to the entire Namibian population and said . . . "say hello to Sam for me". (Sam was Namibia's President) . . . I was entirely awed by that man. I never met Sam.

During the first crime scene investigation I played the dead guy lying over a table bleeding, with a knife sticking in my back. The investigating officer entered the crime scene, surprised at the realism, sucked in air, gasped, "OH my . . . Master Tommie" . . . and pulled the knife out of my back by the handle leaving his own prints on it . . . we convicted him of murdering me . . . we all HOWLED. Damn it was fun to be using my brain again. During one wrap up session at the end of the second day I had a really giant of a cop as my criminal (none of them would play the criminal until ordered by the head man) He was told to be belligerent and obnoxious (totally alien to Namibians, maybe the gentlest of all the Africans) he was reluctant to oppose me . . . Hennie ordered him loudly to resist me. HE DID and I moved him gently, like a helpless child into the next room and they all "ooooouuuuudddddddddd and aaawwwweeeedddddd", applauding . . . I spun around . . . confronted them and yelled . . . . "Do you want to learn that?" They yelled back, "YES SIR" in ENGLISH . . . I yelled, "find me some mats!" I could actually smell my National Judo Team forming right in front of my eyes and knew my new career of teaching English, was not destined for a structured classroom of tired workers trying to stay awake after mining uranium all day.

Hennie, the head cop appeared in dress uniform at my door a week later . . . it was dusk. He said, "Come with me we found some mats" . . . his uniformed driver took us to what appeared to be a large school complex in Venita . . . I saw a sign . . . ENGLISH HIGH SCHOOL and remembered Wotan's words. It was now dark and we used flashlights to enter the school property by key into a side door in the middle of the largest building. When he flipped on the overhead lights I saw the entire floor covered with bright red indoor outdoor rough carpet flooring and felt a drop in my enthusiasm. Hennie saw my disappointment and added quickly "they are sponge rubber on the bottom, walk on it." I did better than that . . . I did a rolling break fall slamming as hard as I could . . . the light and noise awoke the bats. We ducked out . . . me, holding my head yelling OORAH! . . . . I had a whole floor full of mats . . . now what?

The week before, at Ursala's insistence, I had the honor of presenting the newly trained forensic class of police to the local Governor for a ceremony and certificates signed by Ursala for Rossing, The Governor for Namibia, and "guess who" for the good ol US of A. (Oh God . . . wait till the Ambassador hears about this stunt) But it worked, after I mentioned my interest in a National Olympic team to him, the Governor through Hennie, told the school board and the principal we will be able to use them if they are appropriate. At the time I had no idea of the possible political shenanigans or manipulation . . . when the word got around town the crap hit the fan in the white community. They insisted, the mats were bought specifically for gymnastics. I knew there would be rug burns but the sponge bottoms were terrific if you did not slide on bare skin. Hennie and the gymnastic coach met with me and the principal . . . . the cops won! We could start immediately and Hennie would get the word out to the cops in all the west coast towns.

There were NO cell phones, NO internet, only private phone lines, police radio and word of mouth at markets, so, it took an inordinate amount of time. I sat for an hour in a dark freezing cold gym with the bats flying around my head for 6 straight weeks every MON_WED_FRI evening at 7 pm waiting for my first judoka. One night, the door squeaked open . . . It was a cop and his kid . . . I turned on the lights . . . I had a TEAM. Within weeks I had 68 judoka from all tribes, languages and cultures speaking to each other in ENGLISH for three hours a week and loving it. WHO cared if we called it OLYMPIC JUDO. Our first National Judo tournament was in Walvis Baii the following year with five teams from around the nation competing with together. It was announced, scored and refereed totally in English. It was also written up and reported in English in both the coastal and national newspapers . . . OORAH!

Now I needed a plan to introduce Namibia to computers! AHA . . . but first, how do I find a computer . . . ????

Chapter 10

I found out a long time ago I was a strong and very committed believer in ONE GREAT BEING, I never had the problem of disbelief that seemed to bug some of my best friends through my life, I loved religion, it was my mental salvation. I needed it when I was motivated to stop drinking by my daughter Annie. I'm no spiritual salesman either . . . I do not ever suggest what to believe to others . . . that is the mark of a pure CONTROL FREAK . . . . so that's that on what anyone else should believe, this is just a story OK. But I did promise earlier, I would share an occasional insight that I had absolutely confirmed to my own total satisfaction while with my Uncle Connie and the teachers. Since my return, I just can't seem to grasp the idea that everyone is a single person . . . it won't come back, neither do I see social groups or political factions as having any real purpose . . . they all look silly, grown people all huddled together pretending their religion, philosophy or cause will save their day. The only important thing to remember is . . . EVERY SINGLE MOMENT of EVERY SINGLE DAY has been carefully, accidentally, or recklessly constructed totally by YOU. (That was a biggie) That ought to hold your curiosity about what's what in the spirit world for a while . . . then also try to remember every SINGLE SOUL you see or talk to today, is a SOUL disguised as a person!

I have no clear recollection, how I met my favorite African warrior, a German National ex pat, named Nic, "a chermen" (example of his accent). I believe it was when he showed up in the garden at my new partners home in Swakop one day with several ladies in tow, while Jenny served formal tea to all of us in the shade, next to her pond with koi, under a tall palm and amongst delicious smelling flowers and multicolored birds surrounding her beautiful very private home in the middle of town.

Everyone in the area knew I was American Judo, yet for some reason, he continued to brag and brag about his Kickboxing skills, we in Judo never talk about fighting in front of others. He was a chermen brown belt in Judo . . . but, his real skill was as a world contender for chermeny in Kickboxing." I let him talk. I had moved in with JENNY (a great story). She was a full figured (polite old man talk) gorgeous middle 40's blond Brit ex pat. She was a widow, she owned a Namibian rug, carpet and tapestry traditional native Namibian hand weaving business, she owned a terrific home right out of a movie scene, a converted old medical mission, and she was my first attempt to have a relationship in Africa: AND . . . was a totally freaked out vegetarian . . . NO meat or any hint of animal would cross her threshold . . . YUCK . . . but it was her house.

I avoided women . . . especially if they were attractive or interested in me. I could not afford to alienate any segment of the population and I needed more time to train and teach the Judo club I had recently organized. I could not afford to be seen as taking sides. The first instant I met Jenny she knocked me out cold . . . from then on, I could have cared less about MY rules. I never went out to the few bars, and rarely went to Kelly's after hour place . . . I needed to be seen as a teacher and a serious American volunteer. I could not flirt . . . it was terrific . . . I actually liked that part of my life, then I met Jenny . . . but that's for later . . . maybe!

That night, I invited Nic to our regular evening practice Judo session along with his wife and another lady. I asked him to teach my class and demonstrate his world contender Kickboxing skills . . . he was a great teacher; the class was awed and wanted more. I tossed my old Judo jacket to him and confronted him . . . "now show me your stuff dude . . . take your best shot", I smiled and stood totally relaxed, ready for whatever, he lashed a blinding kick at my chest . . . he had a kick like a mule . . . it rattled me off balance backward, I brought my left arm up in a hook type Karate arm block to keep my balance and take the impact of his extended leg against my hooked forearm, his heel hit the very center of my chest. The instinct to block took most of the sting out of it. I held him frozen in space on just one leg. I grinned as I advanced one step INTO him and I nailed him in my favorite JUDO contest throw . . . O soto gari . . . an outer reaping of the opponents leg holding the most weight reaching your own leg extended far behind him, then reversing it quickly, and sweeping his only weight holding leg out from under him. I threw him viciously causing him to slam hard on his back near the shoulders and neck . . . I swept his only standing leg out from under him . . . .

he crashed hard . . . I rattled him back . . . he would not admit the pain, but he had to stop training. I shrugged innocently at the class and parents and onlookers . . . but in true martial arts style, we had established who was in charge, then I coaxed him to start training with us in the Swakop Judo Club and promised to come to Windhoek to help him build his own Judo club. I wanted to start a club everywhere in Namibia so they can all compete together once a year as our Namibian NATIONAL TEAM . . . with Nic aboard as coaching material, we had our National team . . . OORAH!

We became brothers instantly and never broke our friendship . . . EVER! He was loyal to me as Shihan and National Sensei, young and tough, he fought in all the tournaments, took on all comers from other countries, including the Italian National Champion who came to Namibia directly from the Kodokan training mecca for world Judo in Tokyo Japan. Nic became our Namibian Champion. He is still serving as the current 6th Dan international Judo coach of the Namibian National team; they went to the world championships two years ago and took a Gold and Silver recently in the African

Cup, the mandatory African Union prelims to the selection of African Olympians.

We had another South African warrior in our midst. Hein . . . quite a he-man, took a second in a South African Survival reality TV show recently, the only one who could light a fire the old way . . . HE WAS MY MASTER WHEN WE TOOK SCIENTISTS INTO THE UN KNOWN NAMIBIAN WILDERNESS. HE TAUGHT ME EVERYTHING OUT IN THE BUSH. Hein was truly the uncontested all time fiercest guy I ever met . . . everyone is afraid of Hein, he was my hero . . . . and Afrikaner's Afrikaner. Wotan called him "A Recce", and explained they were constantly stationed in the bush for the whole war and could live off of a piece of string for a week (maybe that's a bit over the top, but close); Recce is South African army slang for the fiercest warriors of our time. He lived, fought in, and LOVED the bush. He admitted he was trained by US Marines and Navy Seals and thought I was sent by God through the United States Marine Corps. He showed up at our dojo one night stood silently off to the side scowling as he watched me in the middle of instructing the class . . . it was distracting, but I knew he was important, others who were with him looked up to and deferred to him . . . he watched the entire exercise session observing my regular teaching technique AND the acceptance of ALL COMERS. Would he abide by that in a National Constitution to be written for the admission to the Namibian Sports Council?

I wondered . . .

Could he be the ONE for my replacement, and darned if Nic wasn't a computer expert as well . . . OORAH!

Chapter 11

"Uncle Connie, I sure am so glad you were my uncle".

"Tommie, uncle means absolutely nothing, you are in a true brotherhood, which was formed many many eons ago, long before genetic family or social roles were ever available".

"You mean my current friends are brothers from many eons ago, and are my family and are my true family, not my genetic family?"

"Yes . . . of course, but . . . We see your confusion, you do not choose your genetic family, you have been here as a member of the brotherhood of Oneness many times, in many roles, as both male and female, with; what you are now calling, 'your current friends and family', you all served in many different genetic family and non family social roles"

"Hummmmmmmmmmmmmmmmmmmm mmmm . . . . I'll have to think about that one for a while!"

Meanwhile, back to the story . . .

The greatest double play combination in old time American professional baseball . . . "From Tinker to Evers to Chance", their uncannily coordinated baseball athletic dance, exhibited the timing, agility, and quick reflexes necessary between team members required for throwing out the greatest hitters and runners on the other side. This combination of skills is always the necessary key to any organizational plan of attack . . . or . . . defense.

SO . . . . Tommie, to Nic, to Hein, became its Namibian counterpart. Nic was brown belt Judo, a fierce warrior and a computer expert in real life, Hein was a brown belt Judo, a very fierce warrior and a real expert in fixing anything physical and me, the rookie, an old man adventurer from America, an expert at fixing anything with ideas; what a great combo we were. Hein introduced me to a businessman in Swakop who actually owned a non working computer and mediated a meeting as interpreter where I convinced the guy to loan it to me on weekends. I. in turn would get it "booted" in English, so he could also use it week days. It sounded like a good trade and trading and bartering was our way of life. There were already donated computers in the large government offices, and many were bought by corporations, but few colored or blacks knew the magic of using them (they required typing in English) . . . we had to change this and create newly skilled colored and black workers for Namibia.

I called Nic, he told me to meet a Brit nerd he knew who was on holiday in Swakop, we met at the Bistro for a cuppa coffee (I knew the Guy was SAS). He stayed on in Namibia after retirement from active military service to the Queen and was also an ex pat computer expert. I convinced him "to fix and reboot the computer in English" . . . winking. He winked back and said loudly in English. "You get it to Windhoek and I will take care of it for you, plan on 24 hours for the effort". I took the all day (or overnight) one way train through the Namib desert to the capital the next week, Nic met me at the station, the ride was 10 hours . . . it was very hot, slow, smelly and crowded . . . I loved it, I felt like a true African adventurer.

SAS: So Tommie, what name do you want to be called on your service provider?

WHAT? . . .

What name do you want to be called on your computer address to identify you?

Hummmmmmmmmmm, how about CYBER U @ F%%k you.COM.

Both laughing loudly, I will see if it is available.

I had absolutely no idea what he was talking about.

Nic laughing all the while at my computer ignorance, said "What's a CYBER U dude?"

I explained I wanted to start a weekend CYBER University in Swakop because there was no opportunity for advanced education in English for high school grads, therefore NO INCENTIVE to even attempt to graduate. I lugged it in my lap and on my back on the same train through the desert the very next day, but it was overnight, it took longer, and was much smellier . . . YUCK. I was one happy dude; I had my perfect tool for introducing an American type education to blacks on the West Coast of Africa. Next stop, the Governor's office; we had become close friends, he knew I was working for the Namibian people with no money or sponsor and was seriously connected and well known at the American Embassy. He was glad to have the unofficial personal friendship with me. I told him what I planned, that Wotan, a well known and respected white medical doctor (my Sempei . . . Dr. Wonderful) would help and serve on the board, "WOULD HE, a well known and respected black government leader" . . . I asked.

He shocked me . . . . "of course, if Wotan does I will" he answered. And . . . volunteered to recruit some top white and black Rossing Uranium corporate folks as well . . . . WOW . . . I was hot to trot. Now I needed real American college text books. My lifelong favorite friend Wil Redfearn from our 30'ish Young Republican days was still practicing law in Wilmington, he collected all the out of date law books in his law library and sent a ton of them to me. They are still available in the Swakop library for all to use. Namibia is a Commonwealth country and the common law is the same as in America for the most part. The next coup was my friend Dr. Charlie Johnson from Goldey Beacom College, he convinced a college fraternity to pay the postage and send me all the used text books, used by freshmen and sophomores in the business curriculum and; also recruited a young business student to come over as a VOLUNTEER to Namibia. That's how Nic and I met Martin Mikus. We met him at the airport, he was nervous as hell, we freaked him out on the ride to Nic's farm and had a ball doing it . . . a real ball . . . Martin saw his first African wildlife from Nic's front room picture window. We few, we happy few, we band of warriors, for we are warriors, who started the world's first International CYBER University. It was early 1995. I was on a roll!

*** I just met with Martin, he and his beautiful wife and their new baby are going back to Africa for long term State Department foreign service tour, she is a specialist in AIDS work, and He is an exceptional teacher.

I started recruiting teachers from America and Dubai. I literally dragged Namibian students off the streets to attend college 8 hours on Saturday and 5 on Sunday every weekend. Wotan set up the deal with a movie house for use on Sunday mornings to show a film and lecture . . . it took over a year to recruit, train and organize the teachers and recruit for the first class. Some of my students are on this list now and reading this email accounting just as you are . . . ooooouuuuuing and awwwwwuuuuuing, and should be . . . . they all have jobs and use computers.

Meanwhile back at Jenny's House . . . oh well, what the hell, it's too a good story not to tell . . . . why not???

BUT first . . . I need to introduce you to my young friend Andrew, a South African warrior ex pat I met at /I / Gams catholic mission and Worldteach training center . . . and meet my first new Swakop social friend . . . Peter, a German poet, painter and ex pat . . . Jenny's live in boyfriend!

Chapter 12

'So . . . what's a monad?" I beckoned, TO THE HEAD TEACHER, WHILE ALL SMILED in a beautiful, knowing, loving sensation.

In a sort of what I might call a loving unison of total voluntary understanding . . . I heard, what beckoned to me like a hymn of words . . . not singing . . . . but, an understanding . . . in complete and total unison.

"The MONAD is the organism you call life within all material. It is the intelligence and laws of motion of what you call the ATOM, that always was . . . it began the creation process and is the single energy source for all existence. There is only ONE SOURCE. It is the actual intelligence behind the syncopation of vibration you call Universe, God, Love, Creator or whatever . . . it is the beating heart, so to speak, of the universal vibration of creation . . . .

it is . . . the everything . . . the everywhere . . . . it is the identical universal energy vibration of each individual soul . . . it is your own true self . . . . it is your infinitude being forever."

Wow . . . now that one did take me a bit more time to digest . . . . I have no trouble knowing it, because whatever it is, burns this universal vibrational message into every atom in every cell, everywhere, every second, every day, it is tough to deny its existence and impossible to shake off its memory. Every culture tries to explain this vibrational force. There have been many, many names for it . . . but all agree it exists; and is the ONE creator. AS AND OLD PRIEST TOLD ME LONG AGO. "IT DOES NOT MATTER WHAT WE CALL GOD . . . What we call it never changes God . . . what we choose to call it only changes us."

Ok . . . so now, how do I explain Jenny and Peter . . .

Two pretty young 18 year old British volunteer teachers were stationed at Rossing for a few of the summer months (winter to us). Peter became friends with them socializing at the bars, a rather platonic relationship developed, a well traveled custom in well traveled people, is, that sexual flirtations always screw things up in group living unless it is decided ahead of time somehow to agree on pairs or whatever, but it is required when camping to have an open platonic relationship with all parties. Frankly there are too many sexual predators preying around from the local population, so . . . in a way, he was sort of a big cousin protector OK . . . . that's how it started with Peter and I.

I was a last minute tag along, recruited by Ursala to look after the girls on a planned overnight to the desert area called Moonscape by the locals, to watch a full moon. It was my first camping trip. I had my steel legged type military bed my son gave me to keep me off the ground and away from scorpions and snakes, since he used one like it in his 1983 Beruit US Marines service, I figured I'd give it a shot. so I insisted on bringing it. Peter he-hawed and told everyone in Swakop afterward, I slept off the ground like an American tourist. He never let me forget it. The chess games were magnificent, we were evenly matched, and it turned out that the girls were able to take care of themselves OK. They were scared of their own shadows, every noise was a fierce lion, actually they were geckos, which are loud at night and kind of bark, but no predator wildlife could live in this prehistoric desert wonderland. While Peter and I played chess all night by the full moon, we watched the Southern Cross traverse across the brilliant Moonscape and the African sky . . . it was truly majestic. We spent the next 30 days camping together out there as much as possible and bonding as best friends . . . I still love the guy as he does me, we write sometimes.

He never said much about Jenny, but invited me to her house at night to play chess and watch TV, He told me she was on holiday in England with her mother . . . I never asked about her. I knew by looking around the well appointed home, who the boss of the house was . . . that was enough for me.

A bunch of ex pat tour guides and locals were telling war stories, between beers, about their bush adventures, we were sitting around a big table at the Bistro. Hein regaled them with the story about me getting chased by a lion. I was getting out of our tent one morning in Himbaland, put my hand on a tree, I looked up and suddenly there was a charging lion, tale up, teeth bared, about to eat me. I shit myself, I was frozen in place, and wet from the waist down, the lion's feet landed in right front of mine, and he instantly veered off and ran away. That's the true story. To embarrass me, Hein always tells it like the Tour Guides tell it around their campfires at night, regaling the locals and children and each other while holding their noses. They tell it, that, I shit myself first and the lion ran away from the Americans smell, then they would all hold their noses and howl with laughter. When I protested for him to tell it right, Hein always insisted back, laughing, that "when I actually do something brave I will have my own stories to tell."

Suddenly; "Tommie There's Jenny", pointing, I saw a beautiful blond creature getting out of her Mercedes. I looked down as required of experienced campers and polite bush men sitting with us at the same table. Peter got up and ran outside . . . they hugged and kissed and headed straight toward me inside . . . I froze . . . she had the eyes an angel . . . light blue, brilliant and shining, behind a great smile . . . . I really froze. He introduced me to Jenny. I never heard a word of it. I just shook her hand gently so as to not give off any of the true signals bumping around recklessly within my body and mind.

She sat next to me, when I smelled her perfume I got feint, she grazed my back with her hand and I felt the electricity run straight through me. I was stunned to total silence. When we stood to pay the bill . . . Peter, "Hey Tommie come home with us and we can tell stories. Have a pizza and get to know each other" . . . I felt very nervous . . . "Are ya sure . . . Jenny is just arriving home and all that" Jenny . . . grabbed my arm and lead me out the door, "let's go cowboy". I was totally HOOKED on this delightful creature . . . . aw shit!

The next part of the story has been argued over as to its accuracy many times, the two of them agree and always gang up on me, but here is my version.

We talked all afternoon, had pizza delivered, I massaged Jenny's tired and aching feet, Peter said stay the night, I slept on the floor in the living room, after I gave them a martial arts treat I call Zazen . . . actually it is guided relaxation type of hypnosis, with no particular goal except the one YOU wish to achieve. They held hands in their bed as I talked quietly until I heard them sleeping and left. From then on, whenever both of them planned to do anything, or anytime Jenny was free from the business I was invited, we became tight social friends.

Peter was called to duty for a few weeks as a tour guide and I was left friendless. After a few days alone, Jenny sent word to me in Venita that she was lonely for Peter and wanted to chat. I sent word back; I had no car, so she came by to my Rossing flat in Venita at lunch time. We kissed cheeks politely, she sat and when she crossed her legs I went into deep trance. We both stood in unison walked toward each other and embraced, that first kiss was exactly the ONE we all want to experience and remember. I lifted her gently and carried her into . . . "Man what the hell I am doing???"

We both felt guilty afterward, and made a solemn pact not to make a big deal out of it and avoid each other so as not to hurt Peter . . . what a cad I was, I cheated on my best friend, damn, what a jerk, it was stupid, immoral, I felt completely awful and I could not wait to see her again. She stopped by my flat the very next day at noon . . . and the day after that . . . and the day after that . . . . "Oh my God, what are we going to do???"

OOOPPPSSS . . . I completely forgot about Andrew!

On January 4th, 1994, we, 33 exhausted WorldTeachers arrived in our assigned country of Namibia at the Windhoek Airport after a 22 hour flight and a few days training in South Africa. Our assigned Namibia WorldTeach Superior, an educational and diplomatic guru of sorts met us, lined us up and bussed us to /I / Gams. We were met by the head mission Brother (a Catholic religious order from Holland) and we were told the rules of living together at their mission outside Windhoek. They were easy, flush, and generally keep after the trash and junk created by ourselves in our rooms, dining hall and the showers. The WorldTeach Mother Superior laid down the real law, no hanky panky between the members of the group, be on time and keep the curfew if we are going into town at night after classes, projects or tests.

I saw a suspiciously friendly looking character lurking shyly around the edges of the formal meetings; he did not look or act American, to polite and no false bravado. We both had pony tails . . . mine white, his black and curly, so I sidled up to him on a break one day and introduced myself. We had already chosen roommates and I was certainly happy with Jimmy, but Andrew would have been a likable choice. Very young, 19, very quiet, painfully thin, a South African by birth, a missionaries child by adoption at birth also. He reminded me of my own son and was my close buddy by the time training was complete. When he left for his duty station at Odibo in the north I never thought I would see him again. We spent a week in training there with the others, talk about out in the sticks . . . we were out there right on the dangerous and forbidden Angolan border. On the bus trip at every official check point, we were stopped by mean looking uniformed men with AK 47's and at every new check point they got meaner and gruffer. We were told to chill out and not excite them. But you know Americans . . . yelling at each stop, "hey DUDES where we???" Laughing hysterically at our own immature whistling in the dark bravado until the Mother Superior shouted seriously, as the bus pulled into an ancient mission, "do not go off the paths, we are surrounded with land mines." . . . . not a sound of laughter!

After I moved to Swakop I heard he also arrived there, he had the same type malaria experience I had and was now bar-tending at a local Afrikaner owned tourist hotel. I stopped in to see him, we hugged, shared experiences and were inseparable after that moment, He had a lady friend in Swakop, we spent many hours playing chess together on Jenny's garden lawn under the palm and among the delicious flowers while she was at work, planning a University and telling each other stories about our cultures. I knew him well and loved being in his company for the next 11 years.

Now . . . back to the Jenny and Peter story.

Chapter 13

The whole truth and nuttin but the truth!

Telling the plain unvarnished truth about yourself and coming abruptly out of denial, always hurts, but again, it always feels better later . . . . always, there are no exceptions to this concept . . . so thanks for just being there . . . I truly need to face this stuff again . . . I buried most of it long ago.

After about a week of a fantastically torid and secret love affair, Peter came back from his bush tour exhausted and arrived at Jenny's in his Volkswagen bus, one just like the US hippies drive when they leave their parents and pretend to be fiercely independent. I was so embarrassed by my unacceptable behavior and feeling so guilty I could not bear to go near either of them, I can't lie and knew it would show on my face and body language. They had lived as a couple for two years and had a strange platonic/loving/sexual relationship . . . depending totally upon Jenny's mood. Apparently, she kept the secret about our affair and I was invited to come to dinner on a weekend. (I believe it was a Saturday night)

We all pretended to be the happy foreign ex pat African adventurers joking around during dinner. Suddenly, Jenny turned deadly serious, turned and told Peter directly into his unsuspecting face, she "fell in love with me while he was gone". I stood abruptly, "you guys have a lot of things to talk about, I'm outta here" and left. I walked all the way out to Venita talking to myself directly into MY OWN FACE, like a salty old US Marine Sergeant Major to a raw ass recruit. I was home about an hour, "Knock knock", I opened the door and Peter gave me the biggest hug I ever got from a man. He exclaimed, "You're the new man in the house". I stood open mouthed, hesitatingly, "What does that mean".

He told me the relationship between them was totally over, it was over a long time ago and I was just the catalyst that caused it to come to the surface. I felt better, but still guilty. He said affectionately, "come old man lets finish desert", grabbed me by the arm and escorted me to his VW bus. I arrived sheepishly in the dark garden; Jenny was waiting in the full romance of moonlight and approached me with a real passionate kiss. I turned scarlet . . . the appropriate color for me at this moment. Peter applauded and the three of us hugged a long time. Stunning both of us, she suddenly announced sticking out her hand to Peter, she wanted his house keys took them rudely and grabbed my hand plopped them into it. I stood there with my mouth open. I was the new man in the house. So . . . that's how things are done in the ex pat world, I was truly stunned . . . "where would Peter sleep?" Both glanced as if that was not the problem, after all, he had the bus parked inside the garden gate, right in the driveway. He took a shower and I took a bath and we all went to bed . . . that was the end of that. So I thought!

*** This part is debated often, long after it was all over.

Peter never calculated the loss of middle class perc's on his recently acquired middle class living style forged deeply into his psychic prowess, and the old, 'sleeping in the bus trick', did not last long,

I was not inclined to live in the shadow of Jenny's former paramour and his continued presence in the same house, but I kept that part of me under control. Eventually, after a few days of what I would call "a good try", a joking-kinda slapping act turned a serious vicious raging argument. They punched, kicked and screamed at each other. I sat totally still in the living room out of reach, surprised at the venom and watched the whole deal, it was a sight to behold, and she told him where to stuff his bus and demanded he leave the property that night. I was appalled at the heat the argument generated as they exposed their repressed hate for each other. I was a wreck, now I got him thrown out of his life. Disgusted with myself, I left and walked to Venita. I did not sign up for this drama bullshit in relationships, hell, that's the reason I left America in the first place. I was tired as hell of phony middle class dramatics. Jenny came out the next day to get me and I gratefully accepted the ride home.

Jenny and I really were in love for a time and couldn't get enough of each other, then, as it does with all agreements, when there is nothing committed in writing the whole thing soured. I am not a person that adopts rules or commandments for my life. Being an alcoholic and performing all the screw ups in my life taught me one thing for sure . . . NOTHING IS PERMANENT. I stay loose and keep the sleeping bag and dob kit handy. We were intense lovers for 3 months and lasted 9 more as untrustworthy arrogant and jealous friends. Peter settled his VW bus in a shady tourist area way out on the desert moonscape and started painting furiously, coming into town about every two weeks for provisions, but pretty much out of the psychodrama. One evening, after a year together, as I kissed her politely goodnight, she and I, both started laughing at the exact same moment out loud in a very long cathartic experience, as I blurted out, "you want me to leave don't you", she laughed even harder and as she said, "Oh my God . . . yes".

I moved out the next morning into the two room tiny cottage in her back garden, we, all three of us, spent another year in and out of each other's lives as good buddies, then along came HEIN with his newest African living PLAN.

ONE fine night . . . Hein came to the garden door, knocked and yelled, ""Agggh, Tommie Sensei ". This was our usual routine for many months for our regular exhausting two hour practice sessions many nights a week. I, always waiting, dressed in my fresh smelling clean white Judo Gi, would yell, as I passed by the open windows and doors, wrapping my worn out black belt around my tired old waist as I walked, "see ya Jenny", and meet Hein at the gate. Hein wore me out. He was immediately ready for my plan for Olympic Judo and brought many other ex military types waiting in the wings for any young or old US Marine to show up and provide military leadership and enthusiasm for a cause beyond their currently frustrated and politically unstable lives. The end of Apartheid caused much hurt and much harm, as well as good in Namibia and South Africa., Archbishop Tutu's brilliant move of insisting on establishing "a truth commission" around these parts was the only political shelter they had for their post war life styles, the ability for Afrikaners to make a living and look for work opportunities, as well as, colored and blacks from the losing side was dim at best. NO ONE TALKED ABOUT IT. It is just THERE!!!! I grabbed on to their deep seated physic need and without any real effort whatsoever, except to NEVER talk about it, turned these fanatic patriotic ex military screwballs into JUDO fanatics. They were ecstatic and trained very hard, always begging for more. Hein was here tonight at the gate with more news about MORE

JUDO! "Agggh, Sensei, can we go to the All African Games next year" . . . "HELL YES!" I announced. Now, I could get fierce.

Hein asked if I would be interested in moving from Jenny's cottage into an empty two room flat in the back of his house in Venita for the same rent I was paying Jenny and we could train every day together, he was at the other end of town near our dojo. It was exactly the break Jenny was looking for from my fierce independence. I even ordered meat in public restaurants, a mortal sin if committed in public against a control freak veggie head, that act alone always pissed her off for at least a week. I jumped at the opportunity for personal freedom again. I moved out the next day, we both were very relieved to end the whole matter. I believe our persistent raw honesty is the only reason we are friends yet today.

First we elected officers and such, then as a group, wrote the Namibia National Judo Association Constitution, I agreed to serve as the first President and National Sensei. I was given a life time title of Shihan (father/founder) and the official award of 7th degree for the specific purpose of parity with other African Nations and as a new international activity on the Namibian National Sports Council. I accepted gratefully, I was in the third or fourth degree range in America anyway according to my own Sensei in the States, he knew I cared less about the number. I depended on personal fighting skills for my Judo reputation, he recommended 8th degree because of my unique desire to get a third world nation into international Olympic competition, he insisted, I was the sole sponsor of the effort and paid for the privilege with my own blood. I was happy with 7th.

We established a bank account and I put in a bunch of money I had been given as a gift from America. Hein raised the rest to pay for the trip and we trained as fanatics for the rest of the year. Nic lined up the vehicles for transportation from Windhoek car dealers. He was injured in training and decided not to take up a valuable seat. I trained the entire team as if they were going to fight in the next Olympic Games. Eleven of them had to have black belt certification and international tournament competence. SO . . . I made eleven of them new black belts and proudly gave Hein, our team captain, my own championship black belt from America. We had no adult Gi's . . . only my two and Hein's. Many boxes had arrived from

Tokai University in Japan shipped by surprise months ago, loaded with used Judo Gi's, sent to me by the President of International Olympic Judo Association, but they mostly fit children. Africans were much bigger, but it was a clear sign we were accepted and that International Judo was on our side and desperately wanted Namibia in the bank as the 163rd Olympic National Team, when the Olympic Committee met in France 1996, Hein was Namibia's sole delegate.

I cannot emphasize the toughness of Hein. "Fierce is close". Absolutely NOTHING ever bothered him. He scared everyone in his presence, he actually was what I always wanted to be, fiercely independent, if I can be frank about it, he was my hero. Tough is what you learn to be, when you have no one in your life to depend upon for intimacy from earliest infancy. Therefore, I learned to become independent. Hell, any sissy can be a dependent; it takes real guts to go it alone . . . Tommie Little's lifetime credo. Strange for a person who loves people so much HUH!

"Who's the OOMMM", whispered the beautiful blond South African lady Judo delegate to Hein in the registration line. Oom means, "The old man who looks like your uncle". We had to register our Gi's, make weight, and show our certificates of international competence and lots of other details. We were not one single bit prepared for this international Judo tournament. Finally a friendly face, a coach from the South African police after watching us practice at the stadium, said, "Sensei, you're going to get your ass kicked badly down here," I replied "I know, that is exactly why we came", winked. Smiling. He got it, "Why don't you and your team from Namibia come train with our South African police team at our dojo for the week leading up to the contests". Hein was ecstatic and the others were scared to death. I knew the coach was former KBG when Putin was boss, long retired from the spying game to the coaching game as the SA Judo coach from Yugoslavia, where he was an international champion and red and white belt, I think 7th. He knew, Putin was 4th! Damn small world isn't it. Our blacks, colored and white warriors were adopted by the internationally feared SA police team, we had a fantastic week, they gave us Gi's that fit so we could pass the uniform rules, fed us, befriended us, cheered for us on when we were tired and in all ways bonded as true warriors with our brand new inexperienced scared out of their wits, Namibian team.

The night of the All African international flag ceremony, I cried with pride in the stands watching as our black and white co captains carried the Namibian flag in its FIRST INTERNATIONAL All African Judo Tournament. It was the fulfillment of my lifelong dream. The contestants lined up for the first match, my Namibian judoka threw up right on the mat . . . and that was the beginning of Namibia's international OLYMPIC Judo story. The News Journal Papers headline back home in Wilmington Delaware is my favorite of all. "Namibia loses matches, Gains hearts." I did my job, I was complete. I could dance on a cloud . . . OORAH!!!

Chapter 14

Wham, Bam, Thanks Man

In international pre-Olympic competition, every judoka has to lose two matches in order to be eliminated from the tournament, if you win you advance. My team was petrified, and I mean PETRIFIED into stone when they saw how enormous Egyptians and Moroccans were who were training in the stadium. Egyptians had been world champions for years under Japanese Kodokan instructor trained tutoring. They were scary and very unfriendly. The South African team was scary also, but very friendly. The French speaking countries were tough as hell; the entire tournament was an official language territorial domination fight between the French, English and another one that I forget. The French would not pronounce one word in English, everything was announced three times. The matches began the first day, we got really tromped. Our prize heavy weight, a Mr. Namibia bodybuilder was slammed in 7 seconds after the Japanese command "Hajime" that begins every Judo contest. Hein was the only fight worth watching and he was arm locked by a gigantic Moroccan in the second minute of his first match, he would not admit it, but he was hurt badly. Two of my guys refused to fight the next day. They were so intimated. I wasn't told about the refusal and did not learn of it until much later, I thought they were actually physically injured as they shook their heads when called to the ready room on the loudspeaker and I signaled a pass when their names were called to the mat to fight. We forfeited two places. They were injured alright . . . it was their false pride from being so vocal about being politically tough and full of macho South African patriotic bullshit. Tournaments have a way of sorting out the wheat from the chaff, and that was why I agreed to go to the All African Games in Pretoria. I wanted to let my inexperienced braggadocio Namibian team compete against real African Judo players.

The second day, Hein put up another good fight but was beaten in the very last seconds, things looked very bad for the Namibians. Franz, a

Namibian government sports specialist, trained in Cuba while he was in exile and was promoted up to brown belt by the Cuban coach, he was our last fight of the second day. We had been seriously humbled in front of the whole wide world of Judo. I sat on my assigned chair on the edge of the mat as coaches do and anticipated Franz would get a good beating. He fought to the entire time limit, and then when the referee raised his hand for the final decision and pointed to Franz . . . we exploded, the entire stadium exploded in applause and stood in a standing ovation, the Namibians won their first international Judo match . . . OORAH. The crowd loved us . . . we arrived and survived. As the tournament wound down on the third day of semi's and finals, everyone got social even the Moroccans and Egyptians, we were invited to many African countries to compete and I judged the trip to Pretoria SA a huge success. We all returned triumphant to Swakopmund . . . and were totally committed to a dual match with Zambia, coached by the legendary "Father Jude" from Victoria Falls, the real father Judo in Africa.

One day I heard of a new guy in Windhoek who had been trained for many years at the Kodokan Judo Center in Tokyo, Japan. He was claiming to be a big game hunter from Italy and an Italian national Judo champion and teachers of teachers in Judo. I then heard later, he was visiting Swakop. I found him at the Swakop Casino and Hotel with a tourist hunting group, loaned him my spare Gi and convinced him to come to our practice session and teach that night. He did . . . he really knew his Judo, I was totally impressed. Work permits are impossible for foreigners in Africa and other third world countries, the theory being if there is work for pay, give it to the locals. I won my work permit by working for free and it was well known I never took money from anyone for any work performed in Namibia. He thought somehow he could be paid for Judo and offered to teach me, that was mistake # 1 for Enzo the Italian. His second mistake was taking me on as an opponent instead of as a friend.

Hein was sold on Enzo's Japanese Judo training techniques and they soon found a way to work together in business as tour guides. I saw Hein distancing himself from me at practice sessions. Hein was no longer listening to me as the leader. One night, only Enzo and I showed for practice at the Swakop dojo, I knew Enzo wanted a piece of me in the worst way. I always avoided the confrontation;

Age 62 is not a great age to be taking on all comers. He bowed and said "Randori?" (a free fight used in practice sessions). He was 30 years old, very large, in terrific shape and very skilled. It is Judo custom that when a lower belt challenges you must fight or concede. "Shurrrrrrrrrrrrr" I said smiling, I bowed back and he grabbed my Gi, we fought like two bulls for 10 minutes with neither getting a clean throw. Finally totally frustrated at not being able to teach a teacher, he stood back took a real deep breath and attacked me with a left side O soto gari, Frankly, I saw it coming and prepared to go down hard. I did and it hurt! I stood smiled again, bowed, thanked him for the Judo lesson and left the dojo. He was the new teacher, I quit!

The students started complaining to me about his teaching and training techniques he was rude and condescending to all participants except his favorites, and they were few. I continually refused; all masters know there can only be one Judo master on the mat at a time. In one year as national leader he destroyed everything I built. No one was training anymore except his few flunky's and favorites, plus a cadre of heavyweight wrestlers he recruited from the University of Namibia.

It was national tournament time again, this time organized by Enzo and his buddies to be in Windhoek at the University of Namibia. Nic and other judoka around the country begged me to return to coaching and at least enter a Swakop team in the meet. Hein and the others following Enzo constantly belittled my decision to begin a brand new two month effort to train and field a beginners Swakop team for the event. They were so confident the old ones did not enter the tournament to give the ones they taught for a year a chance at medals. I dragged guys and gals off the streets and trained them every week day in my own Judo fighting style BOK JU KAN, Japanese characters for Simplicity, Gentleness, Instinct. My adopted personal code, my adopted personal style of living, my way. During the two day meet, Judoka trained by me were all in the finals and WON EVERY MEDAL IN THE TOURNAMENT!

I told Nic later, "Screw Enzo and his show off ways, I'll fix his ass." I could teach fighting and I knew it. NOW everyone else knew it and could never deny it. It was a beautifully victorious day for believers in my fighting style. After the tournament there was no argument who should teach and coach the national team. I committed to begin training a national Judo team again. I called a national meeting, forced a vote, won and returned to teaching again on the mats around the country.

*** Oh yeah, Mistake #3 . . . I forgot to tell you about Enzo's and Hein's biggest mistake.

In order to get paid under the table in Namibia in the tourist guide business (like many ex pats) he needed a valid reason to get a visa stamp/work permit extended, so early on he set his sights on Judo as his way. Very clever huh! (BIGGGGG Mistake)

I helped him when asked for help, as any decent Sensei would. I knew he could never get a work permit on his own without me conceding my head man spot to him OFFICIALLY, hell, I knew all the Ministers and they knew me, and he pestered me and finally insisted Hein tell me to write him a personal recommendation endorsing him as the head coach to the Namibian National Sports Council, with copy to the Namibian Ministry of Home Affairs. He knew I would NEVER refuse Hein any thing.

I told them to construct it exactly the way they wanted it, also, to run it by a lawyer for format and suggestions . . . when I got the final draft back from Hein I typed on my letterhead and mailed it special delivery. I did not tell either of them, I added at the end of their letter, Enzo was not now legally employed and expected to be paid somehow for his services. Enzo was ordered immediately to leave the country 30 days later or be arrested. I acted very surprised when I got the news from Hein . . . Oh My God . . . your kidding me!!!

Always remember the well worn principal . . . Old Age and treachery, can defeat youth and arrogance any day of the week! Actually, in the end, I did Hein a favor, He and Hein had to split up the tourist business over the visa issue and Hein ended up with Enzo's new SUV which was their only asset. If Hein ever reads this story he might even thank me.

Anyway . . . as we used to say in the Corps . . . . Wham, Bamm, Thank you Man.

OORAH!

Great read Folks—Former State Rep. Tommie Little continues with his Nambian experience—HOWEVER . . . I'm Warning some of this next email is rather graphic, risqué and definitely far out in—Chapters 15 and 16—Enjoy.

Jud

Chapter 15

"Highlights and Hints about Karma"

"I was thinking about my own Karma just now . . .

My last story about Enzo's "Karmic pay back" got me to wondering about the liability of delivering Karma to others, so, as usual . . . I asked the "ONENESS". I talk to "IT" all the time now, so do you, whoever you speak to, as a sense of higher power or prayer is ONENESS," it "is all the same ONENESS no matter what name you use or "who" you call "IT" . . . so chill out and talk to "IT" like you talk to your very best friend because "IT" is your very best friend . . . give "it" a private or personal name. (it works for me.).

My question was . . . . "Well what did you think of my pay back choice", shortly after writing the Karmic payback story . . .

"Very clever, and you probably saved your friend another lifetime to pay back the debt to his karma for cutting off your personal mission . . . that is the ultimate in forgiving Self, . . . as you like to call it . . . that is, if he handled the acceptance of the event with understanding and without resentment".

HEY DON'T LOOK AT ME>>>>I just type these answers as they come . . . and read the words like you do. I change very little and struggle with typing the foul language and insults I am urged to use, but we all have FREE WILL and we don't need that . . . . DO WE . . . BESIDES, if you have read this story this far . . . you're hooked on your own Spiritual drama like I am; and can't wait to see what comes next!!!

SO . . . . READ BETWEEN THE LINES . . . . WORDS ALWAYS HAVE CONSEQUENCES

*** I remember asking the teachers about this Karma issue over there . . . and here is my best shot at explaining the main points . . .

On the permanently connected side of our individual consciousness (the Oneness on the other side) . . . there is a permanent record created by "all ideas that turned into action" (Lawyers all over the world call this "INTENT") . . . ancients called it the akashic record or the Hall of Records, or what knot. The famous Sleeping channel in Virginia Beach, Edgar Cayce used to read from Akasha twice a day while in deep trance doing thousands of personal life readings with nary one mistake for over 30 years after discovering he could do this BY ACCIDENT while under hypnosis. (read "Many Mansions "or "Many Lives, Many Masters", for a decent and accurate introduction to the subject of OVER THERE) . . . any way without getting technical and all mushy and preachy about the subject, many of YOU already have had an OTHER SIDE experience much more impressive than me. I'm a piker compared to some of you, I have also met many masters both here in the States and around the world, and they all say the same thing about the creator. There is ONE. I purposely went out of my way to meet with many of them and to read about them. So I am bias about ONENESS ok . . . don't forget that.

KARMA is as real as a STONE WALL, after it is created by your idea turned into action or reaction, you cannot ignore it or wish it out of the way . . . and the shock of all shocks to me personally was finding out . . . ideas, thoughts, professes of personal or groupie belief, purposeless drama and needless suffering, unless for the specific benefit of another . . . sucks!!!! . . . and . . . it hardly blips on the Karmic Radar . . . it is self serving, self imposed and therefore does not register as an action or reaction directed toward to another. it counts as neither for or against you. Soul development is exclusively based on ideas turned into action and reaction with others . . . just like the Man says . . . "do unto others" . . . or . . . "you will reap exactly what you sow". There is NO escape from your own actions.

Andrew, Andrew, let me tell you about Andrew. We did so many amazing things together for so many years with absolutely NOTHING to work with, that when I look back on it, I think of the final words spoken by the wild west victims saved by the Lone Ranger and Tonto in the old radio and TV shows . . . "who was . . . that masked man". Andrew was my very best workmate in Namibia; everyone knew it and many were envious that we had such a close friendship and mutual warrior psyche. We could read each other like well rehearsed actors in a long running play. I'd think it, he'd say it, He'd think it, and I'd know it . . . kind of relationship. He was a great friend and fun to be with as well.

So . . . where can I begin . . . ?

"Don't walk off the paths, the place is surrounded by land mines" . . . that's where is really began. Odibo, our training center at the protestant mission in northern Namibia along the Angolan border. I was exhausted after six weeks of being the only old man around these young pups in WorldTeach. The bus stopped at every 'check point' and 'take away' along the northern road for at least 15 hours. I watched the youngin's pretending they were absorbing the real culture. Andrew smiled at me often as I rolled my eyes when they imitated the African customs and handshakes with the staff and each other that they were learning along the way. He spoke the African languages perfectly; no one knew that but me.

As the bus pulled slowly into the mission, Mother Superior barked her orders of the day and we exited. When the locals saw me exit the bus they applauded and an old white haired man rushed me, hugged me, saying in English, "Welcome Father". "Tate" is the accurate African word. He hugged me hard and took my hand, led me by the hand like an old African friend around to meet all the local dignitaries introducing me as his special guest, paying no attention to any of the others on the bus who were all agape at my automatic acceptance in an unknown African village setting. I looked down at the sand and it was actually moving . . . MOVING I mean . . . covered with ANTS. I walked quickly after his introductions into the eating hall with the others stamping my flip flop covered feet full of ants, Andrew was laughing very hard. “WHAT!” I said. He said, “He is the local Sangoma, (witch doctor) he told all of them you are an ancient African warrior spirit come back to help them in their struggles “. I said, “I am? how come these damn ants don’t get it “, in my smart ass American fashion, laughing back. That is my earliest memory of Andrew. Skinny, young, vulnerable, shy, painfully quiet, extremely intelligent, knew all the languages, just the right kind of roomie for me and TA DA . . . his parents were missionaries and lived there. They were on holiday in the south . . . I could get a hot water shower . . . OORAH!

My personal assignment was in one week to get a group of non English speaking high school kids to put on a show, poem, play, and game, anything IN ENGLISH. I decided to have a Judge, Prosecutor, Defense, Criminal (no one wanted that part), and introduced the idea of a jury . . . it was a hit, very funny and entertained the entire village . . . the kids made me proud. All my life, I was always the object of intense personal jealousy by associates. I catch on easy and was always picked for the best jobs and then the leadership. I do not have to study and always paid and earned my own way in all my education endeavors up through and including graduate school and law school. I got elected twice to public office, learned my own hard business and sports lessons, had no family name or financial estate to fall back on, AND could really piss people off. I am very aware of it and very sensitive about it. When I sense it forming I try to let it pass . . . but this time, screw them all with their fancy schmancy ivy league education degrees, they had no clue I went to Bloomsberg State Teachers College and was actually trained as a teacher. I reveled in ecstatic glory watching my team perform . . . . while the others looked rehearsed, rote and childish, MINE COULD ACTUALLY SPEAK AND UNDERSTAND ENGLISH and their parts in the drama, both for the parts they played and the concepts of the issues they learned presented spontaneously in ENGLISH with no memorization of words whatsoever . . . we knocked em dead! GO HUSKY'S!

The last night, we stripped off our tee shirts off, bared our top halves and dared mosquito's to bite us as we did every night, while we paced back and forth walking briskly around the well worn paths, avoiding the edges, (mines are real along the Angolan border), debating the position of the stars in the Southern Hemisphere, the waxing and waning of the new moon and life in general. The long week at the mission ended our formal WorldTeach training and I never saw Andrew again until after we both had our bouts with the most dangerous African killer . . . cerebral malaria, neither of us knew of each others near death experience until we met in Swakopmund.

Swakopmund is a beautiful quaint German colonial well constructed tourist town on the west coast of Namibia. A holiday refuge of sorts for the burgeoning new Namibian middle class of white business and professionals and newly returned from exile black government workers in the new democracy. It was a temporary relief from the rigid poverty and pervasive starvation common around the rest of the country. Poverty is easy to hide. Starvation isn't, everyone everywhere is HUNGRY. Food is always at a premium and hard to get to the desert areas. Most of it comes from South Africa, along with the AIDS virus, brought by the same truck drivers that bring all the other supplies up and down the African continent. They convince women along the way, who they buy sex from with a pittance of food or treasure, that Jack Daniels Kentucky bourbon whiskey cures the AIDS sickness if it is poured over the penis prior to insertion into the woman, then poured directly into the opening used for sex after the act. I can tell you this is the true story of how the AIDS virus spread so quickly along the truck routes up and down the African continent. When the UN passed out condoms in the north the population used them, but snipped the ends off so they could feel the ejaculation happen . . . . NO KIDDING . . . I did not believe it either . . . it is a true story. AIDS is now the uncontested #1 killer in Africa. However, ignorance is still the main cause of death in all third world countries. I was not ignorant; I knew a lot about AIDS, I did a considerable amount research on the subject back in Delaware long before it caught on as an international pandemic terror.

more later . . . about the cure for AIDS."

Chapter 16

"How the Aids Cure Finally Worked"

"In 2008 . . . In Germany, last winter it was reported widely by worldwide press that a gay man with infectious, full blown AIDS and full blown leukemia consented to have a blood transfusion with fresh cord blood from a newly birthed placenta, with the specific medical purpose and singular medical intention of curing his leukemia. Cord blood is pure stem cells and has worked as a cure for leukemia and other cancers in the past for many years. Amazingly, to the shock and surprise of the research team of German doctors it also cured the AIDS virus in his blood stream. He was totally AIDS free immediately after the cord blood transfusion . . . it proved an exact point I had been trumpeting to the medical community, AIDS community and general public in America since 1987.

Back in old 1987 . . . .
"Cure For AIDS"
By Mark Nardone

Now in 2009 . . . Mark a special and very close friend of mine who is currently working as the wonderfully creative writer and EDITOR of Delaware Today. A flashy, upscale, newsy, chatty, monthly magazine—we all read in Delaware to learn what the other guy's pretence life is all about. I met him many moons ago in the middle 80's when I was pushing the CURE FOR AIDS agenda and he was with a local weekly news rag appropriately named BIG SHOUT. I was impressed that he actually cared enough about the subject to put in time and effort and even more important the significant investment of professional and personal reputation into the project, because NO ONE ELSE cared a flippin damn about the issue . . . it was the OTHER guys problem and besides, they were all gay anyway. (The News Journal absolutely refused to mention it). He was like the reporters that busted Nixon; he was everywhere talking to everyone. I know I can certainly bite into some weird and unpopular public issues, but this one was my total and complete downfall and shunnnnnneeeedddd me out of the political scene and social action forever in Delaware.

I actually had the pizzazz to go on local television for seven Sundays in a row with only crossed fingers and pure balls and broad-casted "Conversations with Spirit" for Sunday morning one hour interviews. I did a special one on Mother's Day. I had the freakin guts to put a billboard up at the main political intersection at Delaware and Union fer God's sake, no wonder all my friends deserted me . . . Yikes I would have tooo . . . I also thought I was damn near—if not really nuts! BUT I followed that urge that you know is correct to follow knowing information should be shared. My source of information flow was unique. It started with my elderly next door neighbor as simple amusement in the form of reincarnation therapy—then different past life personalities started to come through . . . I wrote a book about it . . . NO BODY liked it . . . mostly everyone made fun of me . . . Pete Letang my prosecutor buddy still says it was the worst book he ever read . . . it was . . . I agree and I love the guy for being straight forward and breaking my balls. Jane Herrman, was Delaware's own living channel She was an old lady lying on a couch under deep hypnosis, a voice not her's, and without any personal awareness from her stating that there was in fact, a cure for AIDS. Now who the hell would believe a crazy thing like that . . . I DID!!!

Public television show . . . Live on camera: The beautiful gentle voice from the OTHER SIDE, coming through Jane, out cold, in her only good purple dress—said plainly, "Yes Tommie, it is known that the "essence" (stem cells) of the cure for this disease, you talk about. It, the essence, lies within the human placenta . . . it will cure most mammalian blood related problems, as well as cancers" I went to University of Delaware library the following day and researched the well respected and well known "Lancet Medical Magazine" issues on file and BINGO . . . I found it!

There was a complete documented work up and scientific study reported, paid for and supervised by the Center for Disease Control in Atlanta Georgia of 100 women, pregnant with twins from all over the world, suffering from full blown AIDS (actually three had triplets). At birthing day, 203 babies were born. Most (2/3 rds) were totally AIDS free, the only ones who were infected were the first ones through the birth canal. The research concluded they got it through skin abrasions against the mothers bone and body tissue and subsequent mixing with the mother's blood on the way out, clearing an AIDS free zone for the second and third births. Now you would think that fact alone would get the attention of the American medical community at least . . . Naaaaaaa!!!!

I was asked to serve on the Governor Mike Castle's "Blue Ribbon Commission for AIDS" . . . I brought it directly to them at the first meeting. They included it word for word, in the official report to the Governor . . . Naaaaaaaaaaa . . . . so much for government commissions. I appealed to my personal friend Senator Herman M. Holloway Sr. to put in a Delaware Senate resolution commanding the State Health and Social Services Department to investigate the possibility of this cure under the simple common sense theory "He may be wrong, but he may be right". It passed unanimously, Naaaaaaaaaaa . . . . so much for the bureaucracy. I sent it to Magic Johnson and the kid that was on national television who contracted AIDS from a transfusion . . . Naaaaaaaaaaaaa . . . . NADA! NOBODY gave a hoot or a DAMN, and the easier conclusion for my friends and family was Tommie

Little went boonkers. I was totally frustrated, broke and depressed . . . I had spent all my time and money on this effort . . . I quit. I'm outta here!

Finally, I decided it would work in a third world country if they knew about it and immediately started the process of joining WorldTeach so I could take copies of the Nardone article and research with me. I showed it to the Ambassador in Namibia at a private meeting; he blanched, stuttered and told me if I even hinted about this subject in Namibia I was OUTTA there! Naaaaaaaaaaaaaaaaaaaa!

So . . . here I am in 2009 writing remembrances and chuckling like hell over the German success story, meanwhile the AIDS pandemic took over the world since 1987 when I unearthed the CURE . . . now there is not enough cord blood to go around to all the infected victims . . . so much for AIDS education in America and who knows maybe I am a bit boonkers . . . . Naaaaaaaaaaaaaaaaaaaaa!!!

Now I'm thinking again and that dear ONES is always dangerous for me. I am surprised at my enjoyment and gloating about such a serious issue, I am ashamed of myself for that, I knew better, I was taught better than that by Uncle Connie and the Teachers. But then again . . . we really do have free will, and there is no harm in refusing an urge you think is coming from a higher power . . . OK. just being honest. I am going to finish this as a book . . . Friends have encouraged me and I continue to send to Jud . . . the Name will be Letters to Jud . . . the true story of an AMERICAN BUSHIDO.

You are always welcome to say "delete . . . enough already" . . . I totally understand . . . HOWEVER. . . . I hope you will stay aboard . . . you are my audience for whatever is driving my hands on this blasted key board . . . OORAH!

Chapter 17

The Brain Drain

I have often heard the expression BRAIN DRAIN and always thought I understood it as a social/economic/political concept. Simply stated "the smart ones leave and the dumb ones stay behind to run things". That's wrong . . . it is not even close. You do not see the brain drain happen, you feel it later, and it takes a long time for brain drain to settle in, when it does, it is pervasive. The rot of pervasive ignorance adopted by those slowly left behind becomes the norm, then by default of opposition, the standard. Everyone lies about everything, lying becomes the accepted answer to everything, Lying over and over until it is accepted by the community as an innocent ritualistic repetition of their own silly myths. (ie: Santa Claus, the Easter Bunny and the Tooth Fairy). That's a roundabout way of sayin, they believe their own bullshit. And remember . . . 'it's always the other guys fault . . . . "they" did this to us. Then "They" . . . call each other names . . . and . . . "they" ain't very courteous.

Throughout the history of the entire human race during seasonal migrations, men left home to find food or work, if they got it, they asked their families to follow . . . ergo, villages, towns, then CITIES. Population centers all over the world got to be very crowded this way and Namibia is no exception. All human survival is about work for food and shelter. Where there are no jobs, there are no people. Those left behind in depressed areas die a slow death from the reverse of growth . . . called DEPRESSION. The young sense it first . . . "Mom . . . I want to go away to school, this place sucks, there is nothing for me to do around here". "Well not too far now sweety, we want to see your pretty face once in a while".

Use that same combination of social/economic/political facts and apply it to a conversation in a third world family, "Mom I want to get the hell out of here, there are no jobs and nothing to eat ". The third world parents know for certain "NO WAY YOUR GOING, WE WILL NEVER SEE YOU AGAIN".

Well, That's Swakopmund in a nutshell. I watched my friends in Namibia suffer from this destructive malady, with no opportunity except pretense, NO JOBS, no schools from which to get jobs, no jobs for the well educated, no training for the uneducated, no boyfriends, no girlfriends, no future for anyone, especially nothing for their kids, YET, everyone in town pretending today is their most exciting day of their life and their preferred existence.

This brain drain reality hits all social and political institutions all over the world not just Africa, city and farm area school districts die, political parties die, corporations and family businesses die, religious and social movements die, even entire countries and civilizations die.

"What this town needs is an opportunity for computer education after high school", say I, to my buddy and Sempei, Dr. Wonderful, over coffee, knowing his own two young adult sons were in the same brain drain frame of mind and targeting Australia, Wotan got it! It was already too late for his family goals, but he was sympathetic to the entire Namibian community and therefore, agreed to help me put it together and serve on our Board of Directors. I approached him first to start a Cyber

University in Africa for two locals we both knew personally; they were mercilessly caught in the squeeze of the brain drain in Swakopmund.

Sure Swakopmunders could go to the University of Namibia in Windhoek, 250 K away, but there are still no jobs in Namibia to absorb University graduates . . . so . . . I had the enlightened idea to help them stay in Swakopmund and many more like them. I would try to launch a new computer education project in English. Wotan accepted, my next visit was the Governor's office, he agreed and the rest was up to a borrowed computer, Andrew and I. Now I had to sell Andrew into going to college, "Hey Andrew let's have a cuppa coffee at the Bistro", is exactly how it started, and he brought along his girlfriend Juanita (pronounced 'yawn ee ta') She was on lunch hour. She had a job in a beach front tourist hotel office because she could speak, English, Afrikans, German and some Ovambo, but more important, she could type. She was also interested in furthering her education. OOOKKKAYYYY . . . That was our exciting beginning. I now had two brand new willing college students . . . and . . . not one other damn thing, hell I was lucky to be eating after I paid my rent.

There was a computer software firm of sorts in town. I visited unannounced and they politely spoke English to me, then Afrikaans to each other, most of them do that, it always irritated the crap out of me, but I was taught early on to totally ignore incoherence and ignorance as just the other persons way. I talked to the boss about training locals to use a computer, he got it also, he encouraged a beautiful young Afrikaans lady to volunteer on behalf of the company to help us unhook the computer from our SAS business man friend and set it up each weekend in my new flat near downtown, which I planed as our new class room, then return it Sunday nights and re-hook it at his business.

Saturday mornings our Afrikaans lady taught our first Cyber University class of 22 Namibians that spoke very little English and compensated for that small disability in at least a dozen different languages while hooking and unhooking computers, Andrew and I screaming constantly, "if you don't speak English you can't help" . . . everyone wanted to help so they tried . . . . GET IT. It took many months but she did it, we accomplished exactly the goal we set without telling them, they practiced typing in English constantly and all passed a professional

Internet based typing test in English and could send an email in any language, as well as, search for women's fashions, motorcycles and all kinds of crazy stuff I gave them as assignments. Both Andrew and Juanita learned to type in English by ear as I dictated. We wrote all the courses together and put together all the printed materials for the classes, they were terrific students and became my first teachers as well, by the end of the first half year. We had a great time putting it all together . . . here's how we did it!

Chapter 18

Judge me or Judge me not

In the interest of complete and full disclosure, I am not enamored by political correctness, control freaks, and other forms of personal denial and bigotry, so when I speak to these issues . . . I am totally biased . . . I can't stand those people, they suffer from being weaned to late in life.

In the late 60's when I was in the Delaware State Legislature, I sensed the intolerant numbing of America coming . . . everyone I knew thought it was very fashionable (and a display of personal prowess and intelligence) to insist upon correcting the way others think and speak, then they began censuring political opinions of others who disagreed with them with insulting and snide personal remarks. When I returned from Africa 4 years ago I felt people wiping their political correctness all over me like a smelly, dirty old oil rag, leaving my skin crawling. It was obvious political correctness, control of others and personal ignorance became the weapon of the low self esteem. Political correctness . . . . (official speak and official think) is the first sign of the slippery road to National intolerance and numbness, the first clear sign the sociological BRAIN DRAIN has taken hold. When I left for Africa, people were listening to the opinions of radio and TV talk shows to get their daily fix on the latest word in politics from hucksters. By the time I returned these talk shows were considered to be the last word in just about everything. AND . . . when the regular guests call in . . . OH MY GOD . . . they are absolutely awful, They hate everyone for everything.

You have got to be especially stupid to buy into political opinions promoted by the politically correct control freaks and talk show hucksters. I became very sensitive to this issue when I was in Swakopmund . . . their version of political correctness included racial and language groups openly hating each other. And it was macho to brag about it in public. The Germans loved hating the Afrikaners, Afrikaners loved hating them back, both loved hating colored and blacks, the blacks were against the colored and the local black languages were against each other . . . If you came from another country you could cut the hatred in the air with a knife and never figure out who was who's side, especially if a job, money or opportunity was involved. That part was totally YUCKY! But I handled it . . . I kept my big mouth shut and tried to like them all!

So in that testy political/sociological climate . . . this is how we did it . . .

After coffee together, the first stop for Andrew and I was to visit the very hotel chain Juanita worked for on the Mole to get permission from her boss for her to attend school Saturday mornings. It was critical we recruit the first class with a specific determination be in the same class room together two days each week in order to force them to speak English. The head man for the hotel chain was South African, "Aggg, no way man . . . your CIA". I was amazed but not surprised at his excuse to not approve a free education for his employees and immediately went across the Mole to a beach front restaurant . . . "Aggg no way man . . . you're CIA", and so it went over and over, I was at times,

MIA with my family in Delaware, a mob lawyer in hiding, in the US witness protection program, hell, I was amazed at all the different reasons I was in Africa. NO ONE believed I was simply an American volunteer; Volunteering to help people for no pay was not acceptable in their politically correct, control freak consciousness. It was incredibly difficult to convince anyone that, one old man, with no assets, would do the things I did within their community for no pay, and especially with no visible means of support and no particular hidden agenda, except to see folks advance their lives and job opportunity by learning English.

I spent a month soliciting members of the business community up and down the coastal towns about training employees free of charge as future computer workers, "Hey I'm Tommie Little, I trying to start a school . . . etc", "Agggg, man, Are you training blacks'" "YES" . . . SLAM! "Hey . . . I'm Tommi" . . . SLAM, and so it went up and down the coast. I had many politically correct doors slammed in my face, but finally I got the point across to a few good hearted souls and the word spread slowly about the free college education in English being offered on weekends by an American volunteer in Swakopmund. What surprised me most was the determined resistance to the idea of teaching English to blacks by the white establishment, they seemed especially angry that the school was free and therefore available to the general public and accepted anyone who applied "first come, first served. Before this opportunity came along, anyone wanting advanced education after high school had to go to South Africa, England, Europe, Australia and America . . . . and rarely did graduates ever return.

Finally I got my third student, Cooksie, one of my top Judo players. He got permission from his employer to go to class every other Saturday and I agreed to work out a private computer project for him with his employer to type in English and send emails. I had met with Cooksie and his mother privately at my flat one night much earlier in the cyber school game. He had 6 million American dollars of "black" money in a bag. The US sends big amounts of cash money to third world countries that is coated black and requires a chemical to "un black" it. He wanted to sell it to me . . . I howled. It is the second oldest Nigerian scam in the world and he fell for it. I did not break his bubble and told him he could bury it under the braii (fire pit surrounded by stone) in my back yard for safe keeping. (my way of getting it out of circulation). He did, I forgot about it, but I had him by the short hairs he became a student, he lead me to a fourth student, and so it went until I recruited 44 . . . knowing half would not show on opening day. I hit that number right on the mark. Opening day 22 Namibians showed up for class . . . right in front of the Swakopmund Senior Secondary School, or "4 S's" . . . if you were local.

At 8 am Saturday morning the crowd of 22 newly confused languages gathered outside the 4 s's high school. Andrew panicked because the Principal refused to give us the key at the last minute. He had promised we could use a class room on Saturday and Sunday (who ever thought of using a school on weekends). He got serious pressure from the education community as we got seriously organized and gained popular support for the free school. "Screw 'em Andrew lets go to my flat down the street" . . . that's how we got our first Saturday class room. When I moved in, Hein had given me a large round table with 8 chairs and a sofa seating 4, they took turns sitting on the floor. The movie theater for Sundays was the second coup and that was Wotan's brilliant idea, he liked American movies. I used Danny Di Vito's movie,

The Renaissance Man as the first presentation to show how American military slow learners learned English by practicing Shakespeare. The Last of the Mohican's was my next preference in order to break the popular third world myth that Cowboys and Indians were running America.

I recruited old friends from Delaware to send me a steady stream of random thought emails, Ted Caddell was the first one on the team, as were many prominent lawyers and teachers I knew in Delaware. A former magistrate turned corporate lawyer, was traveling to Dubai regularly and visited us three times in Swakopmund for 10 days each, he was our first cyber teacher. We used the Thomas Capano murder trial as the motivational juice necessary to keep the students interested in law and legal issues, Ted Caddell and Larry Nagergast from a Philly newspaper sent their daily professionally filed news stories to me at the end of each trial day and the class printed them out and memorized the names of all the lawyers, players and their part in the story. I had them play different parts of the different roles in mock trial in English; they were invested in the characters and had their favorites. Tom Capano was definitely not one of them. My Africans know every bit of testimony presented in the trial as reported by the two reporters. We had help understanding the case from a retired Judge turned Corporate executive, Josh Martin, he helped us as our school legal adviser, commenting occasionally by email on evidence introduced, procedural issues and lawyers antics in the trial. It was the best teaching experience I ever had . . . I really miss it.

Next we . . . . oh damn, time to stop!

Chapter 19

Eating Forbidden Fruit

Eating forbidden fruit can leave a really bad tast in your mouth, but it is fun, so here goes.

If don't get kicked off this conservative email network for my attitude in this letter I will never be . . . OR . . . . I will know for certainty that my conservative, liberal and middle of the road (like me) warrior friends, are indeed truly spiritual warriors (Bushido) and can handle truth and strange new ideas with tolerance and understanding. I am soooooo tired of the establishment' promotion of only the phony political dogma, spewed out by frustrated cranky old men and one or two cranky women in public forums, on radio and TV talk shows.

The establishment's version of political correctness is clearly immature at best and HOOOOKKKKYYYY at worst cleverly designed to inflame an immature and totally KOOKY audience for fun and PROFIT. I'm 73 years old and know well all the problems of an aging population. I assure you no one in their right mind should be running anything, anywhere at my age. Politics, government and business is a young person's game and even more important, is entirely a young person's responsibility, it is their future not mine. We old farts must rest a bit, read new thoughts and ideas, refresh, make love, make whoooopppppeee, who knows what evil still lurks within us naughty old folks . . . . don't write us off yet, AND . . . more to the point . . . . we are the best political, government, business and education advisers anyone could hire or assemble . . . SO . . . do we do that in the US . . . Naaaaaaaaaaaaaaaaaaaa!

Here is a perfect example of our insistence on political correctness in this century gone seriously wrong . . . . ?

Recently the entire nation watched in living color as a true political revolution happened that caused a blatant sociological, military, financial reality check on the status quo ideas and political correctness. It caused "the IN's" to instantly become "The OUTS" in a flash of predictable massive voting power. I watched this political revolution happen brick by brick in Delaware for four straight years, working daily right in the thick of it. When I returned to my home State, I advised the Republican party leaders formally in meetings and then informally in emails ad nausiam that they were going to get killed at the polls in the next election . . . no one paid a damn bit of attention to the real political issues flooding into the psychic consciousness of the voters, because they were not paying attention to the ordinary folks that vote, they were to hung up on their own arrogance of power, special interests and irrelevant social and bedroom issues . . . bingo, bango, bongo, they went down like a stone thrown off a cliff . . . will they admit this fact . . . Naaaaaaaaaaa.! That's an example of the future of all forced political correctness . . . it is simply habitual error compounded daily by habitual denial . . . It is hilarious to hear it preached by the losers and even funnier to watch the losers trying to convince the public they are still in charge of running the country because their ideas are the right path . . . ooooppppps I'm having too much fun, gloating . . . BUT at least I deserve an . . . I TOLD YOU SO.

Books . . . we need BOOKS . . . . how do you run a cyber University without text books.

After about a year and a half passed in Namibia I went home on a short visit to see my daughter Kelly Little—marry John Hughes, from a well known Wilmington political and educator family, whose father was a sorta friend from Republican politics. I say sorta . . . because Republicans have a very hard time delivering personal friendship. They are the epitome of political control freaks and require a weird loyalty oath to their weird brand of political correctness, at least in Delaware. I don't know about Delaware Democrats they were always very friendly and loyal to me as personal friends . . . . but I sure do know about Republicans—I was one most of my life. If you ever disagree with them on any public or social/religious issue whatsoever they turn into raging elephants on the spot and NEVER FORGET. Nice people, but . . . oh well, you know exactly what I mean; it is well known these days.

Anyway while home for a few weeks I met Dr Johnson from Goldey Beacom College, where I was once an adjunct professor of English for foreigners in the school. We went to the Back Burner in Hockesson for lunch rehashed old times and hatched a plan to make Namibia a sorta third campus . . . how . . . by getting the business fraternity to adopt our school and send their used college texts for the first 2 years of the business curriculum to us by snail mail over the ocean. They took months in transit but arrived at our post office one fine day in great shape. Now I had to teach every college subject required in Freshman and Sophomore year until I had taught someone else to take over a class . . . meaning, I personally taught 9 straight hours on Saturday and 5 on Sunday at the movie house. Andrew was a fast study, quick and bright as all get out . . . he took over the Psychology and Western Civilization courses after the first semester . . . he could teach better than me and knew all the languages, Juanita focused on the computer and typing skills . . . we had a team . . . OORAH. Things were going very smoothly and the town was slowly awakening to the idea that computers were here to stay and cannot be ignored much longer as a reality in Namibia. Beside we showed it was easy, anyone can learn.

Judo was flourishing, Koichi, from the official Japanese Fishery Delegation to Namibia noticed us practicing in our dojo one night and joined us as an older (40) well trained brown belt from Japan. That fact alone inspired the whole nation to take me serious. Someone, I do not remember who, convinced me to challenge the real father Judo, coach of the Zambian team to a dual meet . . . that was a real bush experience. Can you imagine in your wildest thoughts traveling from Philadelphia to San Francisco by crowded car through the wild game parks for one Judo match . . . well we did exactly that. It was hairy but we got there in one piece in the middle of the night at the Capuchin monastery in Zambia. Tommie, yelled "Father Jude," as I walked into mass the first morning, at 6:30 am promptly. The priests and brothers all knew Father Luke, the man giving me the last rites when I woke up from the malaria coma. The day began with introductions all around . . . then off to the dojo . . .

Chapter 20

"It is the LITTLE things that count."

Life seems to be organized around the small, seemingly unimportant details . . . it is always the little things that count the most . . .

Last Saturday I drove to Pottsville Pa, to attend St Patrick's Church for my cousin Bobby's 50th anniversary as a Maryknoll missionary priest. He was always my true hero . . . all the time we spent together growing up, he was my model for a guy to be like, and it almost worked. I announced my intentions to be like him in my senior year of high school at North Catholic in Philly.(The Oblates of St.Francis De Sales)

To every one's surprise one day I announced, "I want to become a priest". Bobby heard about it from his mother and he sent me a daily prayer book from his Maryknoll seminary school in the pine woods in New Jersey. I opened it, damn, it was all in LATIN, I flunked Latin, OH MY GOD, I'm cooked. That did it, in that very instant I knew full well I would scandalize not only my family but the entire world of Catholicism.

I was late for the Mass and when I quietly slipped in the side door, I saw the entire crowd for what they really were to me for the first time in my life . . . the Deweys and the Reileys . . . all in the same crowded church at the same time for the same reason to celebrate together the success of one of us. BUT I saw them as my family. I never saw them like that before; I realized at that moment it took a whole village to raise me and my brother, the family orphans. It was GREAT. I began to tear up; I finally knew I had a real honest ta goodness family. I was in foster care as a youngin and lived with all of them at least once in my young life. I was stunned, they were not appearing to me to be my old grey haired cousins anymore, I saw them only as they really are, my brothers and sisters . . . even their kids are my brothers and sisters . . . WOW the tears built up and I wiped them secretly, smiled and waved at everyone looking at me sneaking into the pew.

*** That is exactly how I felt the on the other side with Uncle Connie, at first I was stunned to see we are all family, even those we think we hate as enemies are our family. Suddenly, It was embarrassing to be truthed naked in front of all, to admit I had hurt my brothers and sisters while taking sides on this planetary tour as a hitch hiker; and worse. I realized there are no score cards kept and no gain or advantage for good behavior or what we are conditioned to think of as social gain . . . nor does being a goodie nor being a badie count for much either, only how you treated the other guy when acting or reacting together. Possessions and titles accumulated count for zero, nada, nothing . . . all we possess over there are the final results of our ordinary daily actions and reactions with our neighbors. Did they cause heavy karma, light karma, good karma or no karma at all? I will freely admit . . . loving your neighbor is the most difficult spiritual challenge facing all mankind.

My man Cooksie, 4 am, Swakopmund . . . "Sensei, time to go". He had driven 26 miles up the coast from Walvis Baii and was knocking on the window of my flat on the edge of town. He had with him in the car, Lawrence, his brother, Quinton and another I forget. We were to pick up Andrew and others and follow in Andrews vehicle, drive 400 k or more to Tsumeb in two crowded sedans to our heavyweight's Schultz's home at the center of the northern mining country way out in the sticks, the other end of the Universe, to meet the rest of the National Judo team. That will take all day; we will stay the night at Schultz's, that's the plan. After an hour of patience . . . finally I exploded, "DAMMIT . . . speak English, what am I invisible, speak English if I'm in the car or let me out, OK, you're making me crazy" "SILENCE . . ." this was going to be a LONNNNNNGGGG ride to Zambia.

I remember bodies lying all over Schultz's house in crumpled sleeping bags the next morning. I was awarded a bed because it was an age thing. I loved playing the age card in Africa, all the cultures actually respect age and it is an honor to be the old man, not like back in the US where we are made to feel we are inconveniently in the way. We decided to leave Andrew's ratty old sedan behind because it probably wouldn't make the trip through the veld anyway (bush talk for wild country) and take Schultz's newly borrowed mini van and Cooksie's fathers new sedan and head east toward our target . . . the Zambian Judo team. So here we are 10 Judo players and a coach covering every competitive weight class with no spares, crowded into two vehicles with our sleeping and personal gear heading east to our first international Judo meet and really psyched. We traversed the exact same path from Swakopmund I had taken to get back from the Guinea Fowl Inn in Katimo Mulillo in the Caprivi strip with the cops; we passed the gravel road prisoner scene as we got nearer to the town near my first bush duty station. I was floored that Freddie the Innkeeper remembered me so quickly, he glanced up from his desk as we entered the Inn and ran to hug me . . . "Master Tommie, it is so good to see you."

"These guys are my Namibian National Judo team Freddie, proudly waving my hand around at the team standing behind me, "I told you I would do it". "There was never a doubt, what can I do for you". "Can we camp out on the lawn tonight, money is very short", patting the pocket of my faded maroon bush jacket, that had become my trademark, "OF COURSE you and our Namibian team are my guests". We pulled the vehicles around back to the lawn where I first practiced Judo with my friend Michelle, the Egyptian Judo man who saved my life. We parked the sedan next to the back porch with the van behind it and planned the night's sleeping arrangements. No one could sleep outside on the actual ground, the Zambesi crocs love to attack at night.

Schultz started the argument when he casually suggested the Afrikaners could all go to his friend's house to sleep, I knew they would party a bit and see us in the am hungover that did not bother me one bit. It would also require we cram the rest of our team into one small sedan that bothered me a lot. I balked, "If you guys sleep inside tonight, they sleep inside tonight ", pointing to the colored, blacks and Andrew. Andrew was silently on my side of the conflict. "I will use some of this money we pooled together to pay for the two rooms." patting my pocket again, they balked and whined until I pulled the wad of bills from my pocket waved them around and swore I would throw the money into the Zambesi, leave immediately and hitchhike back to Swakop by myself if they refused. It is commonly known by anyone who knows me well, I NEVER MAKE A FALSE THREAT, hell my own kids would easily attest to that. They yielded immediately, grudgingly left for the party and the rest of the team got to sleep indoors. I slept in the exact room where I began my African life in Caprivi . . . . "GOD help me . . . this is going to be a very long trip".

Stopping and sleeping out on the ground in the veld during the next leg of the journey through the game parks would be totally INSANE, Lion were everywhere. We had to be careful just to take a pee in the day time . . . one of us always watching out in the open The game sightings were awesome, elephant, zebra, giraffe, all types of four legged, cheetah, wart hogs, you name it as they sniffed casually at us wandering slowly past our vehicles. We in turn, respectfully waited for them to pass by, especially the herds of elephant brushing their tusks against the vehicles. What a sight, it was amazing. I kept hoping, "One more leg in the journey and we are there!!!!" Then, we hit pothole city . . . the African North South truck route, I hate to tell you what the pothole jolts felt like . . . you could hide a Volkswagen in some of them. However, as I said before, we arrived safe and sane, at the monastery in the middle of the night, slept a few hours in real beds and even the protestants went to mass early as a tribute to Father JUDO our host. After a great breakfast with the priests and brothers with introductions all around we showered and dressed in our Gi's for the bouncy trip to their dojo in the capital.

Chapter 21

The Most Dangerous Judo Match Ever Fought

Father Judo and I were in the lead vehicle, he instructed us that he knew where the worst potholes were and was familiar with the crowded territory around the Capital of Zambia, "On to Lusaka", he pointed, "Follow me", the others followed in a caravan. I soon saw, what looked like a scene from a Discovery Channel. Africans everywhere sitting and lying casually on top of moving vehicles, strolling back and forth on both sides of the road, pushing carts, carrying everything you can imagine on their heads. He pulled over to a news boy on the side of the road to joyful happy cries of "Father Judo, Father Judo", took out a wad of bills larger than mine and asked for a paper, stating that he "knew it had a story in it about the arrival of the Namibians ". I looked surprised as he gave the entire wad of bills to the news boy, "what's that all about?" He whispered conspiratorially out of the side of his mouth, "I better buy it now, it will be more expensive by this afternoon", I said, "why", INFLATION, he quipped with a grin, finger to his lips as if to hide from BIG BROTHER.

Judo is a 100 plus year old Japanese sport developed in 1882, admitted to the Olympic Games in 1905, created and developed by Dr. Jigero Kano, so that, he and his prize physical education university students could practice an ancient form of personal combat known as ju jitsu. Judo is the greatest self defense system ever developed by the human race, anywhere. What makes it unique is the protective break—fall Dr. Kano developed to protect the one being thrown from injury. Therefore, throwing can be practiced intensely in training. Learning Judo is all about patience and balance and timing, no more no less, and when being thrown to fall correctly. Mats are critical. The entire international culture of sport Judo is practiced in the spoken Japanese language; therefore serious Japanese ritual is involved, respected and expected by all countries everywhere.

We arrived at the dojo about 9 am in our fresh Judo Gi's and were treated as celebrities among rounds of applause from the Zambians along the streets. Our team was awed and very impressed by the attention. When the formal line up began inside the dojo, they were wide eyed with pride. Father Jude had convinced Japanese Judo to send its best teacher, a 6th degree from the famous Kodakan Judo school in Tokyo to Zambia to train police and coach the National team. He was about 35 . . . tall, wide, very polite and pleasant, wearing his red and white ceremonial belt. Father Jude was 4th degree. I felt like an impostor with my politically correct constitutionally awarded 7th degree and was shy to show leadership. The formal line up was my very first; I am a tournament fighter, not a ritualistic performer. It was personally embarrassing to me to be kneeling in the top place of honor with these two great international Judo players kneeling formally on either side of me. Both national flags were raised to national themes of music and my team of different cultures and languages were very teary eyed at the sounds of our Namibian National Anthem as it played over the loud speaker when the Namibian flag was hoisted over our heads on the mats. My heart was beating like a tom tom; I thought everyone in the dojo could hear it.

We would repeat this formal ritual again right before the actual tournament fights begin, but this was a ritualistic tribute from the Zambians to my team for traveling so far and was a great motivator for all. Now, typically we would practice together four hours each day, for a few days and learn techniques from each other. The Japanese coach was confidently wandering around the mats teaching and instructing everyone. I was shy to interrupt him and lacked the personal confidence about teaching my American Bushido fighting style in front of him.

He was comfortably showing Namibians some arm locking and choking techniques that I recognized as standard Kodokan Judo, his defenses were as well. In response, I let it be known I was also available to the Zambian team for randori (practice fighting) by strolling into the center of the mat and lifting my open arms, gesturing to no one in general. A large Zambian approached me aggressively and bowed; I bowed, gently pulled on his left collar with my right hand and reached slowly for his right sleeve with my left hand. IT IS NOT ACCEPTABLE ANYWHERE TO ATTACK A SENSEI, so I was very relaxed. At that very instant, like a lightning strike, he spun into, "what a layman would call a shoulder throw", you have seen it many many times in martial arts movies. One man swings a punch, the other ducks under it with his shoulder into the armpit of the aggressor, then while turning his back, quickly lifts the aggressor up over his shoulder high into the air and slams him on his back into the mat right at his feet . . . Get the picture!

As my surprised 61 year old feet left the mat and my surprised wrinkled old face was lifted way up into the air going in the direction of . . . over his shoulder . . . I put my free hand on his back . . . shot my legs straight back instantly at right angle with the mat, even with the floor, shoulder high . . . his spin stopped dead in its tracks as he toppled backward like a fallen tree, his feet flying up in front of him, so that the force of the fall was on his two shoulders and neck. We both slammed into the mat at exactly the same instant. He on his back, me on my stomach, my hand still clutching his collar in a vicious choke from behind, he was pinned tightly on his back. We landed with such force it knocked him out cold. Father Judo blew a whistle, everyone starred . . . I thought OH OH . . . I blew it! He and the Japanese coach conferred—heads bobbing in intimate conversation, then whistled again and assembled the entire Zambian and Namibian teams around us lying there. They all started applauding and the Japanese Coach insisted immediately, "Sensei, please teach defense". Bowing in English with a heavy Japanese accent, "How you do that old man???" GRINNING WIDELY.

No one on my team had ever seen me do anything like it before. They had never seen me attacked, and I only ever used it in a serious self defense situation where I am under attack by surprise. It was pure old fashioned US Marine Corps "kick their livin ass ju jitsu!" It is not in any Judo or self defense book, nor have I ever seen anyone else try it. I invented it when I was very young Marine—training with my team at Parris Island, SC under Sensei Jeff Nadeau. I learned to kick out my legs from my experience in gymnastics and diving. I was middle—weight in competition and in a habit of training with any heavyweights I could get my hands on. It worked beautifully on big guys, because of their naturally slow telegraphed spinning movements. The timing has to be perfect. I nodded to the Coach from Japan that I had much more like that, and was asked to demonstrate all my secret defenses to the Sensei from Japan. We became Sempei and student in an instant of recognition . . . it was a glorious three days for American Bushido.The Zambians never attacked me again and they especially loved my sneaky double foot sweeps.

*** Father Judo took me aside after the formal introductions the first day and quietly announced half his Zambian team were infected with full blown AIDS. I had a team meeting immediately and told them the danger of getting blood on them in a fight and that I have no intention of putting them at risk. The Afrikaners were highly enraged . . . “Agggg . . . we came all this way to fight Sensei . . . screw AIDS”.

We kept a squirt bottle of bleach handy on the side of the mat to squirt immediately on any blood event when it appeared in practice or in a contest, but that is not by any means fool proof, AIDS can live up to 20 seconds outside the human body and can get into the tiny-est. cut or scratch. From that moment, I was totally convinced Afrikaners are the toughest, most fierce fighters I ever met, and had hearts like lions; anyway, they won my heart and the argument that day in Zambia. Every team member agreed with them and we went on with the meet with extreme caution. The referee’s were vigilant . . . that is how Namibia got through the most dangerous international Judo contest in Judo history. Oh yeah, we won four individual matches . . . but, it was Zambia in the end with the total team points. Headline back home in Namibia.: ZAM beats NAM! I would have settled for . . . Namibia loves Neighbor.

BECAUSE, “Love your neighbor”, was certainly put to the reality test in Zambia. We loved them and they loved us . . . THEY WON . . . . OORAH!

Chapter 22

January 1998, I turned 62; I had been in Africa 5 years and had some petrifying and joyful adventures. I had been back to visit the States twice, once for my daughter Kelly's wedding to John. It was well done as a nice normal middle class church going family affair. The problem was I had gone native, did not go to church and did not relate to anyone in the middle class anymore. I can't remember why I came back from Africa the second time, but do remember it was also a nice middle class church going family affair, but again, I was off the charts with my insistence on personal simplicity as my life style and behavior guide with my only social clothing being barefoot, jeans and bush stuff.

Suddenly, I got my annual attack of malaria and spent about three days on the floor at my daughter Ann's house in Brandywine Hundred. I was used to staying at my friend Jane Herrman's house because it was my official voting address in Wilmington. I was so damn lonesome for some comfort food and familiarity and desperately needed TLC badly. (tender loving care) I was sick as hell and could not stand Jane's dark, depressing, and lonely old house one second more. Ann came through and invited me to use an upstairs bedroom in their home to hide in and suffer the fevers and shakes in private. I loved her kids and I got on just fine with her husband.

I was still miserable when the fever left, I was wearing bush sandals in freezing winter. Hein convinced me out in the bush that living in bared feet prevented colds and infections, besides I was broke and had no shoes. My daughter Annie bought me a pair of desert boots to take back with me. Honestly, everyone I met was terrific at trying to make me feel at home. SO it wasn't them, it was me. I had no interest in ladies or dates of any kind and was thinking I will never be connected ever again to a real woman personality. Frankly, I could not wait to return to Namibia after each visit.

My friends had bought, lock, stock and barrel, into the pretense of upper middle class materialism, their politics became conservative, their social habits routine and predictable, their aspirations uncreative, boring and all about how many material things they had accumulated, their religious and moral values were totally false, talking one way on Sunday and doing another on Monday and that totally turned me off. I knew I had no family anymore after the divorce and that I was not welcome in any type family scene. Everyone I met was pretending the situation was normal and very much OK . . . . it was implied at every social brush, that it was me who was the strange one in the mix. I could not get on the plane fast enough.

Long before my decision to go to Africa I had been divorced (1987) and it hit me very hard, as it does everyone else, right in the pit of the stomach, I pretended I could care less when it happened and beat my chest like all the other guys. What really bothered me most was not the separation from my wife of 27 years, I eventually figured that out and accepted that we just did not like each other very much and staying married would have been a total disaster, hell, we could not sit in the same room without serious tension, and the kids took her side without even trying. So I gave all my friends and family up as part of my future.

What really bothered me the most for the longest time, was the separation from everything familial and therefore, familiar to me. I was only divorced from one person but, that single act immediately separated ME, from my personal history that belonged solely to ME. My life was MY history . . . . the only history I had of ME. In conversations I was hearing, I saw that I had already done all the things that they were admiring in their new social chums but none of it ever worked for me, PLUS, when I did it, it was always considered the wrong thing to do. I was clearly a man without a personal history, I had become invisible. I got depressed in the States and when that happens I do something about it . . . . I QUIT . . . . I scrammed outta there early after the second visit; truly convinced I could create a new personal HISTORY for myself in Namibia. I actually hated being back in the US, I felt guilty about being free and different from the others, always having to fake liking the things everyone else liked and were constantly bragging about, everything was measured in $$$$$$$$$$, to me $$$$$$$$ was just plain boring, simple as that. I knew I was destined to live out my life in Namibia and started planning my new personal history.

Hein picked me up at the Windhoek airport; we were excited driving through the newly green desert, after a month of the Good Rains. I felt as if I came home and we planned the next few years of Judo. We both wanted to be in the Olympics in the very worst way. Andrew met me at my new flat, excited I came back early. I no longer lived at Hein's, and we planned the next few years of our brand new creative Cyber University, I was happy doing something important and everything I was doing was going very well . . . then It happened . . . MY WORLD TURNED UPSIDE DOWN.

It was the following Sunday about 2pm, right after the last class of the day students were still talking together and hanging out, Juanita and Andrew were putt-sing around with the computer teaching others to tear it down and giving instructions.

KNOCK KNOCK . . .

I opened the front door and there stood the most enchanting, beautiful, dark haired, green eyed, young Afrikaner girl I may have ever laid eyes on, rocking up on her toes shyly, "Hi I'm Danielle, can I go to your University?" "Smiling in total wonder,

"Come in and look around, These are the students, here is the computer, here is the class room", and I bragged a bit about the work they were doing that made me so proud. She walked around looking fascinated at the idea of starting school and said, "When can I begin." I replied, "Next weekend!"

At the front door, "Now . . . What else can I do for you Danielle" smiling.

"Well," very shyly looking directly into my eyes, "I always wanted to marry an old man".

Half joking, extremely puzzled and totally hypnotized, I never missed a beat, "Well honey you sure knocked on exactly the right door, do you have a Mother and Father,"

"Yes"

"Can I meet them"

"Sure"

Then to my complete amazement and total embarrassed in front of the others, I bent compulsively and gave her a light kiss on the lips.

We BONDED that very instant. I was hooked.

Talk about May December relationships . . . I . . . turning 62, She . . . turning 17!!!

Chapter 23

"I hear Ya . . . . I hear Ya"

OK OK . . . . I hear ya . . . I hear ya, I know I was stupid, I knew I was stupid the moment it happened, I just plain did not give a damn and NO ONE could talk me out of it. I told her parents that very same thing when we sat down to dinner in the beach front restaurant the next night. I said to her Mother, "I can make sure she is educated and gets a job", and to her Father I emphasized "I was getting social security starting this month and would be able to take care of her as long as I live".

She just turned 17, had become a high school dropout and street kid, living between two divorced parents separated by only walking the distance of the town and neither knew where she really was. I found out later, she was recently in the hospital for a suicide attempt. I also did not know the parents had already checked with a local shrink to see what he thought; he thought it was the most appropriate thing to do under the present circumstances. Anyway, I was determined to take care of her, but was smart enough to insist the parents be witnesses to an official and legal wedding in magistrate's court. We went to the Dad's house for desert and to finish the celebration of the planned marriage. Both knew I would keep her off the streets and that was their prime motive for their enthusiasm, her Dad admitted that to me later.

Now before you go getting all self righteous and judgmental, remember, I knew from the teachers, we choose every single important relationship WAYYYYY ahead of time, we change family roles and come in groups often to complete a predecided mission . . . I knew that. They are not called relationships on the other side . . . they are referred to as . . . AGREEMENTS . . . . made way before we are born. We make AGREEMENTS and come in an attempt to fulfill them. YEAHHH, of course we pick our own Mothers and Fathers . . . and we will actually wait together until the time is right to be born into large groups. Suicide shortcuts the plan and murder interrupts the AGREEMENT process . . . . EXCEPT in the case of committed WARRIORS. We committed warriors accept any form of death as part of our mission, dying for a friend is the greatest of all warrior missions, like the man said, "no greater love, has no man, than to lay down his life for a friend". That's just the way it is . . . I did not make up the rules . . . . ?

Anyway, I was confronted with this notion of a spiritual, karmic mission when I saw Danielle from the first instant; and to make it worse, I was head over heels in LOVE with this beautiful little girl, now what the hell was I going to do, except attempt to do it right. I honestly and truthfully thought it was a childish whim and would be short lived maybe two years at best, but I still insisted we get married if we were going to live together no matter how long it was going to last and she was all for it. Her father and mother and little sister moved her into my flat three days later. I was deliriously happy. She was also . . . we probably set a world record in age difference (45 years) . . . but neither of us cared a twit. So WE DID IT . . . just like my regular, ordinary, middle-class, church—going friends in Delaware. We got married!

The Judge could NOT stop laughing after she sorted out who was who in front of her. Her Mother and Dad, and old Grey haired man and a little girl . . . she said "Who's getting Married to who", in English; and then finally attempted to get a serious look on her face with her head down in the book to carefully read the words slowly in English as if we all needed an English interpreter. The bailiff giggled and snorted behind his hand when I raised my hand to say "I do" . . . the Africans loved it, the Afrikaners hated it, and the Germans were totally enraged. We really hit the Swakopmund gossip circle . . . then I called my kids . . . they were floored. Well I'll be damned . . . they did care, I finally had a life of my own choosing and they were freaked out . . . I told Danielle "THEY HAVE NO SENSE OF HUMOR".

The first 90 days of any love agreement is hormonal and therefore totally exciting. We were no different on that score. However, I could not get it through to her that not holding hands in public was a smart thing to do. She took it as a rejection, I could not help it. The white Swakop dudes were mean as hell about the whole issue and she would eventually get the heat for it, if not now, for sure later. We did everything together . . . She took to the computer like a champion from Microsoft and to reading books like a student. I was in school heaven, teaching every class every weekend with the exception of Andrew's two. Danielle was likable and there were no other flirtatious ladies around to tip the hormonal possession scales. The guys flirted with her, but all of them were respectful. I would say honestly the first year made it a great adventure in relationship, honesty, experimentation, fathering, and just about everything I needed to feel fulfilled as a person . . . happy I was . . . like Ogden Nash said,

"While lolly gagging in the piazza, it was a clam I was happy as a"

The second half of the Cyber University 1st year began, we lost a few students over the beautiful, summertime weather, Christmas holidays, but 18 showed up to register for the February 1 beginning. Danielle made it 19 . . . and Jusso made it 20. He was the West African golf champ, taught at a local country club and the white population absolutely loved him. He was considered the Tiger Woods of South Africa—a big handsome friendly guy, smart as a whip and spoke fairly good English. It was a great start for a great semester . . . who said IT COULDN'T BE DONE . . . . OORAH!

More later from Tommie as our . . .

FORMER STATE REP, FORMER US MARINE, 7th DEGREE BLACK BELT JUDO MASTER, DELAWARE ATTORNEY, GREAT LOVER, WRITER, AND WORLD TRAVELER—TOMMIE LITTLE CONTINUES.

Chapter 24

"Zazen—Using The Magic Of Your Mind"

Competitive Judo was slow that particular year in Swakopmund, my arrogant Italian coaching assistant Enzo saw to that. Wotan convinced me to teach Tai Chi to the general population, which turned out to be a great idea. In Judo we called Tai Chi, "Sissy Judo" . . . or . . . more politely, "Judo without a partner". All experienced Judo competitors are familiar with these slow moving strength building and balancing techniques. We practiced them every day; they are exactly what we in Old Judo call "mirror training", practicing our techniques alone in front of a mirror to maintain balance and consistency in motion. However, no one had ever seen my explosive Tai Chi, preformed purely as a self defense technique when 5 or more aggressive opponents were attacking at the same time. In competitive training we practice it often.

The general theory being; since every motion begins as a circle . . . complete the circle when momentum is in your favor: and change the circle into a new circular direction when inertia begins to wane. Truly, it is that easy!!!

I demonstrated it to the class a few times to prove its effectiveness, Then, at Wotan's insistence on politically correct Tai Chi, I bought a Tai Chi beginner tape on the net and watched it a few times. It was useless, so I developed exercise movements to fit into my own Bok Ju Kan explosive BushidoUSA fighting style, it was an immediate hit, and a crowd began to come and were coming regularly twice a week. Wotan bought us all black tee shirts with the Bok Ju Kan Japanese characters printed on front and Simplicity, Gentleness. and Instinct printed on back.

Wotan, Andrew and Danielle became my best students; they ended up teaching it when I was gone on trips around the country or back to America. The most popular part of my exercise class was always "Zazen", the cooling down period at the very end of each practice session (same as in competitive Judo) . . . everyone relaxed on their back, eyes closed and went into a guided hypnotic dream state for 20 minutes. I never learned it from anyone, I never saw anyone else do it, and there is no information on the net or anywhere else about it. I always knew how to do it.

The word Zazen actually means "sitting in concentration" and is promoted in the Far East as a religious or meditative experience. I just knew how to do it from the very first time I tried it and was a true master of teaching it from the very beginning. GO FIGURE! The proof in the pudding was when my Swakopmund Tai Chi students won all the medals in the National Judo Tournament a year later.

Here is an example of how Zazen works; before the Zambian trip, we trained in Walvis Baii at a municipal community center that had gymnastic mats . . . it was our team's commitment to practice in Walvis twice a week and Swakop twice a week for about six months to prepare for the All African zone 6 competition. Cooksie from Walvis, was injured in a rugby game and sat in the stands two evenings a week just watching for months, his brother Lawrence was on our team, Cooksie was his driver. Cooksie never set foot on the Judo mat during the practice sessions, he just watched . . . but did Zazen twice a week in the sitting position on a chair in the stands while we closed down each Judo session with Zazen as the cool down routine while lying on mats . . . . GOT THAT???

I have a regular traditional Zazen routine I have used for over 50 years for any student or athlete. I have used it in high school sociology class at Brandywine High School in 1964. I used it with swimming teams, wrestling teams, basketball teams, softball teams, and teaching English, including such complicated matters as studying for Bar exams, you name it. I use it to relax the mind and reinforce the proper education goals or training techniques to the athlete or student in the dream state . . . sorta like this . . .

Relax your body . . . (Position unimportant) I am your protector for the next few minutes while you close your eyes and totally relax . . . let your mind evaporate into the Universe. First let your feet relax, then on up the body, legs, hips, trunk, shoulders, neck, arms, face, finally the muscles behind your eyes relax and your alert system is closing down. (that is the key instruction)

"I will count backward from 8 to 1 (all the numbers mean something already explained) When I say ONE, you will wake up in a beautiful natural environment alone, NO OTHERS will ever be present . . . this is YOUR place of BLISS (OTHERS are always the direct cause of and the sum total of all personal stress) . . . you can walk, run, skip, jump, sit on a rock, or just wander around enjoying the aloneness and the scenery, if you want a nice experience put your chin forward, put your arms in back of you like superman ready to push off the ground . . . then bend your knees and push . . . you will fly". (I spend two minutes watching the Rapid Eye Movements)

THEN . . . . In a moment you will change dreams . . . you will awake in a beautiful dojo . . . many black belts are smiling and waiting patiently to be picked by you as your training partner. You will repeat the exact same training techniques you preformed tonight in very slow motion, correcting every mistake and asking your partner for suggestions. then you will pick another partner, fierce, vicious, larger, heavier and do the same exact routine at top speed making NO MISTAKES . . . and so on and so on . . . according to the planned training session goals . . .

The night before a team trip to the South African zone 6 championships . . . he walked to the side of the mat . . . Sensei, can I fight in the championships . . . I roared out loud . . ." You gotta be kidding me", took off my Gi jacket and threw it to him . . . belt also. "Go fight someone dude!!!" He did . . . he threw everyone on the entire team, no one could resist him . . . I was stunned, his technique was perfect . . . he went to zone 6 in South Africa and came home with a silver medal . . . so folks don't BOOHOO Zazen . . . and I have even better stories than that . . . so . . . trust me, I can do major feats with Zazen and it builds terrific stamina and confidence like nothing else I have ever seen . . . OK Ok I admit I'm testy, it's not your fault, I'm edgy today . . . I just get totally bored and tired of the jerks who know absolutely nothing . . . and . . . keep telling me . . . . I know absolutely nothing. Anyway . . .

Zazen WORKS great in ordinary high school or elementary education . . . wait till you hear about the Ovambo 8th grade class in business management at English High School, I have a letter from the principal to attest to that feat . . . but . . . next time folks . . . a weekend is coming up and I am lonely, so expect some more stories from my memory bank about Africa.

Chapter 25

Tribal Wars

This event happened in another of my recent Namibian lifetimes, during another love AGREEMENT . . . Remember Jenny . . .

While we lived together I had a job for 6 months teaching 8, 9, 10th grade business management at English High School. It is impossible to get a work permit for an American in Namibia, but I was dependable, well known and an experienced teacher. My Judo team trained there three nights a week, so when they needed an emergency replacement for a pregnant Namibian teacher, I was offered the temporary job. I was thrilled and really got into it. One day on the way into school, Dieter, my principal stopped me and asked me into his office, uh oh . . . I'm fired already was my first thought. “Tommie, can you handle another 8th grade class . . . we can’t pay you, but it will really help us”.

Hurmp! Typical Africa. “Shurrrr why not, what’s the deal”, “We just got an entire group of Ovambo’s transferred here from villages in the north and they are all living in hostels here in Swakopmund, they have NO English whatsoever and you just have to keep them quiet and do your best to keep discipline”. “When do I begin”, “come with me I will introduce you to them”.

OHHHH MYYYY GODDD . . . they had beards and most were in their 20’s, very shy, tall for Ovambo’s even the women, and all totally bright eyed with PANIC and FEAR. I asked the interpreter with Deiter to tell them I was a famous American lawyer invited to Namibia to learn their unique cultural ways and was very proud to be appointed as their teacher for a few months. He did, and left! I smiled at them, dismissed the class and wondered what the hell I was going to do with them for the next few months. It was Friday, I thought about it all weekend. Monday am, I went into school early and wrote the word ZAZEN on the black board in large bold letters . . . under it, in smaller letters I wrote the word SLEEP!

When the class arrived they were very respectful and polite, I waited until they settled apprehensively in their chosen desks . . . I waited until they were totally quiet and all looking at me, then dramatically pointed to the word Zazen, put my hands in a prayer like position next to my face tilted my head closed my eyes, and made a snoring sound, then opened one eye and pointed to . . . . sleep.

They imitated me and soon were all very much asleep, some snoring gently. I was totally amazed . . . it lasted about 20 minutes. Then slowly they awoke rubbing their eyes very relaxed and all smiling broadly at the relaxing experience. The FEAR and PANIC totally gone from their eyes . . . caused by this strange American teacher. Periods were 40 minutes . . . OORAH . . . I had a plan. I did it every day for the entire week until all I had to do the following Friday was erase the word Zazen and point to the word SLEEP and they all went out cold. The FEAR and PANIC had left their faces entirely by Tuesday and each day they became more and more relaxed and as they awoke they spoke to each other quietly or joked politely with each other during the rest of the allotted class time.

Monday I tried something even I thought was strange. While they were asleep I read to them softly, from their 8th grade business text in English. I read slowly and emphasized dramatically as if they were totally awake and understood English. I was nursing them carefully to learn how to say my words properly. I finished each lesson in 20 minutes, then added, the words, "you will learn to understand my words and to imitate them when thinking about or speaking to me or others in school", then I told them to awake themselves refreshed and feeling good for the rest of the day. When they met me in hallways and after school they always smiled openly and said "Hello Sensei", like all the others kids in the school . . . it did not occur to me they had any idea what the words meant they were saying to me. I just smiled back and said, "HI".

I want to take a break here for a moment and thank from the very bottom of my soul, the wonderful warrior friends of mine out there for their great observations and responses in return letters . . . you make me strong, I truly love you, especially those of you who were enemies of mine for brief periods. Many of you out there are true Masters.

I affectionately call one of you "Sgt. Bilko", he recently gave me a terrific insight and a complete memory trace into my trip to the other side . . . it's a simple insight . . . and goes like this . . . "Hey BILKO . . . I am talking directly only to you, YES . . . there is a sacred YES . . . it is the only true vibration in the UNIVERSE. Every other vibration is subordinate and therefore, totally inclusive, but, none are GREATER . . . it is the sound of GOD speaking if you want to call it that. Saying the sacred word 'YES', is the key to LOVING YOUR NEIGHBOR . . . and that is all I am permitted to say about it. It is not my wish or purpose to appear judgmental." . . . meaning . . . "judge not, lest I be judged", like the man says.

Now back to Swakop, I did this daily Zazen routine for the next few months we were together, they were extremely relaxed around me and some of them joined my Judo practice sessions. The greatest tension in Judo class was getting the different tribes to actually sit next to each other. Finally I just ordered them to fight each other on their knees (so they could not get hurt) and they all ended up friends . . . so much for the Namibian tribal wars.

The whole nation has to take a national educational test each year imposed by someone I consider totally insane at the UN (connected to $$$$$$ given by NGO's) Testing is a totally ridiculous form of educational activity, replacing actual teaching time with a focus on rote learning . . . but that's another issue for another day. I was selected by the University of Namibia staff lady as a paid matriculator for the 9th grade groups during the annual test. I was a cop . . . I watched so they would not cheat. The whole country had people like me marching around watching students taking tests in every school.

Two weeks later as I went to an evening Judo class, Dieter called to me and beckoned I come into his office. I walked over to him casually we had become good friends," HEY TOMMIE, you vill vant to see your krades fer die Ovambo's", "No thanks I only promised to keep them quiet remember." "Tommie, you vill vant to see your krades", "No thanks . . .", I protested again. "CUM you vill see yeeer krades", he ordered. I went into his office he showed me the actual test scores from the Ovambo

8th grade class . . . . they scored the highest "krades" in business management in the entire nation . . . my jaw dropped. YES . . . they took the test in ENGLISH!!!

Dieter Meyer, wrote me an official letter on official high school stationary at my insistence attesting to this entire matter, because I knew damn well no one in the American educational beauracracy would ever believe this story . . . and I still have the letter in my file someplace . . . . OORAH!!!

There is always more than one way for a teacher to skin a cat . . . if you can think outside the BUREAUCRATIC LOCK BOX!

Chapter 26

The Ugab Base Camp

The Ugab Dry River Basin. Namib Desert, Northern coastline of Namibia.

You can't get there from here . . . if you want to try, here is the shortest and best route to take.

British Airways at Philly Airport . . . 8 hours to London, England . . . 1 hour to Frankfort, Germany . . . . 12 hours to Windhoek, Namibia. That part of the journey only took a day and a half, considering the 8 hour layover at Heath Row airport . . . but the shopping is magnificent if you have money . . . and the food exotic. There is a sleeping room and conveniences for young children and small kids.

Now get ready for a 7 hour drive straight to Swakop through the beautiful ancient fossil rich Namib desert . . . baboons lurking everywhere, and four legged horned beasts of all types crossing the highway at dusk, so watch out! Passing through about 5 small mining towns with kiosks and petrol stations, where coffee, food and cold drinks are abundant . . . and please try the strange foods that are normal to the locals.

Aha, finally Swakopmund . . . it comes upon you like a small quaint European town from a distance . . . flat, flat, flat is the horizon on the coast except for the world's tallest sand dunes, especially after driving through the ancient mountainous primitive scenery in the Namib desert, including Spitzkoppe, the most popular camping site in our part of the desert. "Aggg, Hey man lets go camping", is all you need to hear on a Friday night in any decent Swakop bar, we all get our sleepy bags, some wood for fire, food, a kettle and cups, water, coffee . . . and any other substance or musical treats you can carry for the evening's entertainment . . . everyone will bring black plastic bags so NOT to leave trash or beer cans behind. Then OFF WE GO to Spitzkoppe. The colorful sunsets and golden sunrises are glorious.

Where were we . . . oh, yeah . . . Ugab.

The Christmas holiday season before I met Danielle, I had a severe attack of homesickness. Jimmy explained it to me at /I /Gams early on as a desperate fear that "NO ONE WILL EVER REMEMBER YOU", it's the best damn explanation I ever heard. I had been a ex pat for 5 years. NASA experts say you can take aloneness for about 4 years, then ya gotta go home and fuel up on familiarity, otherwise, you will seek new psychic solace, that is called GOING NATIVE . . . . I hope this makes sense to you.

Simply put, you lose the loyalty to the old and begin loyalty to the new, as in The STOCKHOLM SYNDROME. You begin to sympathize with your captors if the aloneness is forced upon you. Being ALONE is not a natural state for mankind. We seek company and take what we can get . . . I was truly there! I was soooo there, I wanted to walk home to Wilmington Delaware, straight across the 8000 mile Atlantic Ocean, and leave that night.

Early in the afternoon, I met Andrew and Juanita in the Bistro, moaned a bit, started tearing up and both reacted embarrassed. Jenny popped into the bar, whispered in my ear and left. I did not react at first and just said thanks as she slipped out the front door. I told both of them she had a call from America. I got the news from Jenny my very best lifetime pal died of a heart attack, my buddy Wayne, we were close mates from first grade communion together all the way through graduation from Northeast Catholic High School. Then a tour in the US MARINE CORPS and then after that, on to Bloomsburg State Teachers College together.

I was sick with heartbreak and loneliness anyway and he was one of my few friends that actually understood me. He knew I was a compulsive leader and never followed the advice of a single soul in any matter whatsoever, he knew me . . . oh my God, how I missed Wayne, and what made it worse was . . . I wanted to go home with him. I wanted to die that instant in the worst way . . . God how I cried!

After a few hours of embarrassed commiseration with them they said, compassionately, "they could drive me half way", to the loneliest place in the Universe I knew of, the Ugab Dry River Basin. I knew a guy that was stationed out there in the real wild. He was managing the Rhino Trust, a British

NGO, saving the black rhinos from extinction. I knew I could find him and throw my sleepy bag on the sand, stay a while and OD on alone.

I figured some alone discipline imposed on me right now would cure my homesickness or at least drive me completely nuts . . . either way was OK with me, at that point in my suffering. I was truly suffering with uncontrollable tears, elevated heart rate, sweats, headache, stomach acid burning my throat, cramps . . . I'm telling you I was suffering. I had to get out of Swakopmund and fast. I had money for petrol and food to go half way and back . . . then they had to drop me and turn back, I would press on alone.

We headed up the Namib Desert coastline, past the magenta colored salt pans, oyster farms and small village of Hentis Baii, along the fierce looking and forbidding Atlantic Ocean toward Cape Cross, the popular tourist photographic stop. A fantastic nature sight and enormously populated seal colony, you do not need a sign post . . . it stank for miles . . . the ride was soothing, bumpy and full of chatter about our Cyber school projects to start after the holiday in February. I began to relax.

At Cape Cross we hung a right and headed east into the desert toward the Ugab Dry River Basin, very bumpy would be an exaggeration . . . potholes and darkness do not mix. We had traveled about 8 hours altogether and came to a small one horse town . . . really tiny . . . I said, "this is far enough let me out here." I waved goodbye, and wondered what the hell I was doing there in the night alone . . . I felt great! I rolled my sleepy bag onto the front lawn of a small darkened motel near the parking lot with no cars in it and stared at the stars all night, thinking about how much I loved Wayne, then how much I loved my family, then how much I loved my friends, then fell asleep.

I awoke with the face of a pleasant looking local looking down at me, with a hot steamy cuppa coffee in his hand, "Master Tommie, what you doing way out here . . . ?", extending it toward me politely, I could never figure it out . . . how did they always know where I was. I gratefully accepted. We struggled with polite humor in English, but I got the point across I wanted to go to Ugab. He understood and pointed across the way to the only market in town and there stood MY friend Paul from the RHINO TRUST . . . he waved, recognizing my maroon sleeveless bush jacket and both of us started laughing our heads off at the coincidence.

The next part of the trip after loading the stores, and a few provisions for me, was another 6 hours driving straight up (or down) the windy, sandy river bed in the humongous SUV owned by the Trust. Paul was a great tour guide and explained the geology, flora and fauna as we bumped along . . . the animals were all out in style to show off their prowess and he knew the history of every one of them, including the birds. I learned he had to come to this tiny town once a month for provisions and today was the day. He also was leaving the base camp early in the next morning and intended to spend a week or so in Swakop on holiday and wanted to get the regular Trust shopping done for the local villagers that acted as security against poachers for the Rhino's in the Trust.

I had been there a few times camping overnight doing tours with Hein and knew all the village leaders, he said I could stay in his own kraal and in his tent (with a real mattress) as long as I pleased and the villagers would enjoy my company as always. At last . . . Home sweet home!

Paul was my next door neighbor in Swakop when I was living at Jenny's, we became good buddies, he had a gorgeous wife and child. I admired them, suddenly they were no longer an item together, he was devastated and acted typically macho Afrikaner style as if he could care less. He hated women this day and it showed, God help the ones he would meet on holiday, his attitude was very aggressive. Anyway we made a fire, said greetings to all the villagers . . . cooked a meal and talked about philosophy till the wee wee hours of the morning in his kraal. When I awoke on the sand in my bag he was GONE.

The dominant village dog was named Mugabe, the village had a good size herd of domestic goats, which were penned behind fencing every night and left to graze most of the day, while two young boys with long sticks kept them in line and assembled them as much as possible as they wandered up the hills all over the dry river bed landscape that had plenty of easy to reach green leaves to eat.

Mugabe was a scarred up old Rhodesian Ridge-back short haired fighting dog, about the size of a large calf, big for a dog . . . he wasn't mean, but protected the goats from leopard, lion, hyena, whatever was hungry around these parts. He had a ferocious bark and I bet a bite as well. He sniffed me up and down as I left Paul's kraal to find my place of bliss far downstream from the village. He kept following me and I threw sand at him until he went home.

If you ever truly want to face your FEAR right in the eye, try sleeping alone in the bush. Paul tried to talk me out of it, the leader of the village, Johannes tried to talk me out of it. They said I would die the first night and the village would have my blood on its conscience. Johannes said leopard were prowling the area, as well as hyena, he insisted dramatically with hand and facial signs signaling most of the conversation, "it was dry up north and the four legged were in a migration mode coming down into the valley for green leaves and water" . . . therefore, "THE BIG TEETH NOT FAR BEHIND, MASTER TOMMIE"

I said something stupid about, "needing to do this" . . . caught myself and shrugged, tearing up. He understood. I left the base camp with my pack and bed roll and trudged downstream to find my perfect SPOT. THERE IT IS my mind said . . .

you always know it when you see it. MINE . . . all MINE. MY HOME. It was lovely . . . a wall of rock straight up to heaven, a large shade tree, plenty of fire wood, I built my braii with river stone, then looked around for my sanitary spot far away from the eating and camping SPOT. You know the old expression "don't shit where you eat" . . . that's what it originally meant, before affairs began in both business and politics.

I was busy all day long, next thing I knew it was getting dusk . . . I lit my night fire, a very big one . . . I wanted to dance around it like in the movie Dances with Wolves. I was psyched, I ate my beans and meat . . . drank coffee slow and real black . . . bush coffee is when you put the dry grounds into the tin cup and pour scalding water into it . . . then top it off with a splash of cold water from your canteen and the grounds sink right to the bottom . . . it is coffee heaven.

I became suddenly aware night had fallen like a blanket . . . I could see absolutely NOTHING past the big camp fire . . . and just as suddenly the wind stopped . . . . complete silence . . . I heard a noise in the brush . . . holy shit . . . I must be nuts. I panicked . . . got out my sleeping bag unrolled it put my Marine fighting knife (K Bar) down deep inside . . . slipped off my boots, and crawled in facing the stars . . . I used a log for my pillow. The stars were incredible, HOLY SHIT another noise . . . OH MY GOD . . . I will definitely be eaten tonight . . . I could not close my eyes and was too scared to get out of the bag to pee.

After what seemed like an eternity of scary hours, I finally relaxed a bit and started praying my ass off. Please let it be quick! Please let it be quick!!!

I heard heavy breathing close by in my right ear and freaked out. I scrunched down imperceptibly slowly into my bag trying to cover and protect my head and reach for the Marine fighting knife at the same time . . . the breathing got closer and heavier . . . it stunk . . . I shit myself.

I felt a fowl smelling light lick on my face and I passed out . . . when I opened my eyes there was Mugabe . . . wagging his tail wanting to play. I jumped up and chased him stumbling in the sand and throwing both shoes after that damn animal. I was laughing so hard I started heaving my dinner, he came back and spent the night lying near me. I love Mugabe . . . we became close pals for the next ten days . . . but damn that dog . . . I could not clean up until morning.

more later . . . about my awful second day alone.

Chapter 27

YUCK . . . I smell awful

Eventually, I actually fell asleep, I laid on top of my sleepy bag after chasing Mugabe, feeling fully protected by my newest very best personal friend. Johannes woke me, he was whistling at a distance for my new four legged buddy and also, at the goat herders in the river basin, there were goats all over the place. He was polite but kept a respectful distance, with my pair of boots dangling from hooked fingers in one hand, sort of hiding them behind him, like he was embarrassed to ask how they got there. I asked him by mouthing words and sign language, how I could wash up and he roared laughing, slapping his thighs at my antics, as I pointed to my backside and held my nose.

He pointed in the direction of Paul's kraal. I grabbed my dob kit, a towel, fresh underwear, jeans, tee shirt and wandered through the sandy beach toward civilization. About 300 meters later, I saw what he meant . . . a primitive shower within a closed in reed kraal, obviously built for sissy tourists. Inside was a bucket with holes in the bottom, hooked by the handle to a hemp rope on pulleys and a lever to open it once it was hoisted high enough to stand under it. A fire was burning under the donkey . . . (not a real one dudes) . . . a donkey is a large 55 gallon drum lying on its side resting upon river stone with a fire place under it . . . you build the wood fire . . . cold water comes into one side of the drum from a bore hole deep in the river bed, while the hot water is drained out from a spigot on the other side . . . WALLAH . . . ingenious!

A HOT SHOWER . . . I cannot describe the feeling of the cleanliness after three buckets full of scalding hot water cooled down by a beautiful shade tree and a light wind blowing against my clean bare skin. Truly the best outside shower I ever had.

Johannes made me understand that the village ladies would consider it an honor to wash my clothes and I accepted gratefully. Damn I turned into a sissy already . . . and I haven't been there a full day YET! When Andrew and Juanita dropped me off I gave them all my travel money, but not my "in case" money. I am a subscriber to Adam Smith's philosophy that "cash is KING", and always keep emergency cash hidden somewhere, about 10 dollars American will get you a week's worth of services anywhere in the bush, and translated into Namibian money it was a fortune to the village. I had folded hand washed clean clothes delivered to my perfect SPOT every morning, they were collected every night. I never saw them coming and going. Johannes forbid anyone to bother me at my tree (notice the claim asserted . . . MY TREE) and he accepted the cash after my insistence and his many protests; on behalf of the entire village.

Honestly, I do not want to write these next words. By noon I got the worst case of PERSONAL GUILT'S I have ever experienced. I had no one to speak with, so, with no stimulation my mind kept wandering back to previous audiences and personal dramas throughout my life. I screwed every last one of my friends . . . I was never honest with anyone . . . never forthright with anyone . . . never fair with anyone . . . I was a total shit all my life. It was the most awful day of personal expunging in my entire life and I just knew it was going to get lot worse as the day dragged on. I bought some fresh meat and drinkables, hot chocolate, coffee, sugar, and a few chewies at the tiny market in the tiny village yesterday . . . damn was it only yesterday . . . seems like a month ago.

I busied myself all day long improving my territorial defenses around my perfect SPOT. Getting extremely territorial moving and rolling large sitting rocks around the fire pit and stacking the fire wood neatly that I would need for my ritual dance tonight, a naked Samurai war dance around my campfire with sparks blowing in the wind, my sword flashing in the light of the flames with the dramatic Japanese warrior music playing loudly in the background . . .

As the day progressed the guilt's mounted . . . I began crying again and again at the pain I had caused all the people in my life . . . I was exhausted with grief. By dusk I was prepared for the night terrors. My four legged buddy came around at dusk as I ate, he would not eat the food I offered, he was a proper real dog, no human being sissy stuff would pass his mouth, he hunted his food, I was so jealous and envious, I was a full blown civilized sissy. I started crying again and begged him with pleading motions and noises to come closer and let me pet his head . . . he would have none of it . . . he was a proper fighting dog, a real warrior. He sat and watched . . . or . . . went for quiet walks alone when bored with me.

After I washed my plate and cup and stuff . . . I built a raging fire . . . fashioned a long stiff stick as a Samurai sword . . . stripped bare naked and began my war dance, something was missing . . . oh, of course, the music. Oh well it worked anyway. I was feeling very tired and sleepy, I put out my sleepy bag under the Camel-thorn tree out on the sand near my fire, laid my head on the log, starred at the Southern Cross, moaned a bit and cried myself to sleep. I slept like the dead ALL night, it was wonderful. I awoke refreshed and ready to attack the day. "Hey Mugabe, want to explore the wild today?? He smiled and said "YES! . . . YOU BIG SISSY . . . lets boogie"

That was the end of FEAR in my life . . . the third day was peaceful, contemplative, full of feelings of gratefulness . . . it was like being back on the other side but still in my body. I began talking out loud to Mugabe as we strolled along casually hoping to meet the elephants. It was as if we were the closest of mates all our lives as we strolled courageously down the elephant walk in the river bed toward the reed sea where they went to binge on tall grass and drink cool water . . . OORAH!

GEE it was great to feel alive again and finally have a real friend, who demanded nothing, asked nothing, would take nothing and was willing to give his life for me. The rest of the ten days was a piece of cake, except for the caterpillars on the fourth day. I awoke with a tickle in my nose and felt my face moving . . . I sat up and was covered with black sqimey things.That got my attention. The fifth I hugged a thorn lined Camelthorn tree trunk for a whole day and reached my second Japanese Samurai personal characteristic. Ju . . . Gentleness. The trick to relating to thornyness in others is "gentleness."

Another day, I do not know which, I stopped counting, I watched a shadow cross a mountain for one whole day, I now had all three characteristics to disipline my self, Simplicity, Gentleness and Instinct, that would be my personal living code for the rest of my life. When I arrived in Swakop, I had it tattooed on my upper left arm . . . the one least likely to be severed in a fight.

I was ready for action . . . bring it on . . . then one day I saw a fancy tourist SUV filling the air with dust coming down the well worn tourist road. I was disappointed and yet happy to leave, it had been ten days alone . . . I loved it, but . . . .

They were Europeans and wanted to know everything about my ten days alone that night around the campfire sitting on my guest rocks in MY SPOT. They wanted to hear everything this old salt had to say about Africa and life in general . . . . I hitched a ride next day with them all the way back to Swakop. Hein was dead right . . . I now had my own stories to tell.

Next day . . . . "Hey Andrew . . . guess what . . . . we are having our final exam for the first Cyber class at the Ugab Base Camp" . . . he smiled, just rolled his eyes . . . I could come up with some real doozies.

Chapter 28

Whew! finally a return to NORMALCY

The Swakop Summer Christmas holiday was finally over and the tourists, the money moochers and the South African hangers-on were all gone. Ugab was the best psychic tonic I ever had, like a dose of salts for my mind and a high energy boost for my body at the same time. I had already met Danielle, who was now the love agreement in my life, knew I would try to keep it, I also knew, that it was purely a total pipe dream that might last two years, if that. School had been in non-eventual session for a few months and Danielle and I were adjusting to the idea that an old man and young girl can actually get along just fine when in-laws and other interfering grownups do not meddle.

Our marriage was planned for the week after my first social security check is deposited in my Wilmington Trust account, it was very late in coming. It looked like I had to go back to the States to straighten it out and again the Calvary came to the rescue . . . thanks again to my buddy John Flaherty and Mrs. Daniello at Joe Biden's office, it took them many many weeks to sort it out, lotsa of emails back and forth and I had to return 6 months of the actual paper checks that were mailed to me by the Social Security Administration, by mistake, so we could start all over again from scratch in automatic deposit. It worked out, we got married and I will never forget the Biden folk's magnificent effort on my behalf.

We had 20 students still attending class regularly, some coming only every other week, like Cooksie, doing special computer projects assigned to make up for time out of class. We used a four person survival team approach to learning everything, with five teams of four students each assigned to work together. Each group of four was made up of the different local languages with at least ONE MEMBER STRONG IN ENGLISH. The entire team was graded together as one unit in every subject, the point being the weakest in English gets help from the strongest so they can all pass.

The books arrived safely and had been distributed, read, and recopied for those who needed time to sort out the English, Andrew and Juanita became great teachers and the computer was going day and night with Danielle now living in our flat (school) 24/7 helping everyone who visited enthusiastically with their homework and other assigned projects. The three of them took to the computer like members of Best Buys famous Geek Squad.

Even the weather was totally normal, as usual Swakop has four seasons during each and every day . . . cool to cold at night, sometimes very misty in early morning, spring arrives around 9 am, summer for sure by 11, fall by 4 and then winter comes again when darkness falls. Americans would absolutely love it here, they can enjoy putting on and taking off their layered outfits four times a day, with an actual reason to do it.

Annually, Summer begins in September, lasts until about February, then Winter begins coming on slowly and lasts until the next August, in Swakop the four seasons come every day, unless there is

East Weather or "Berg Winds" as the old time CHERMANS call it. Think Santa Anna winds if you're from the US. The wind blows steady and VERY HARD from the Namib desert toward the sea, it brings all the sand it can carry with it for about 8 to 10 hours straight. The sand will blast the paint from your vehicle . . . truly. Then the wind stops abruptly for a few hours and the weather turns absolutely fantastic and the whole town hurries to get their braii's lit and the meat cooking and the beer cans popping as the celebration of East Weather begins . . . sounds exciting HUH!

Well if you do that for 6 straight weeks in a row you'll soon get sick and tired of it, at least I did, the malady is called cabin fever. There is not much else to do in Swakopmund . . . generally, winters tend to be very dreary and summers tend to be very hot.

BY THE WAY, surfing in Swakop is the best anywhere on the African Atlantic Coast and surfers come for contests from all over the world. I do not surf it is too damn cold, the water in the height of Summer is still freezing because of the current from Antarctica swinging around the point of the cape and flowing up along the Namibian coast from the tip of the Horn of Africa, but again that is why the fishing is so good and attracts the international fishing fleets. Danielle and I walked every day on the lonely Atlantic beach . . . until we hit a certain predetermined point then we'd turn and walk back . . . everything was completely quiet and NORMAL.

Tai Chi was going great Tuesday and Thursday nights, I loved meeting and talking with my Sempei Wotan about life in general. I was reading books I had always craved to read and he was constantly giving me a new one with a different point of view . . . we discovered Dan Brown long before the rest of the world . . . and debated the truthfulness of the Di Vinci Code often. It did not get any better than this . . .

The Ugab final exam project was taking shape . . . the students were totally in charge. I was orienting them to business so they could meet the business community in person and some day get jobs in town and what better way to advertise their skills than to let them plan for a budget, then beg the business community for the essentials needed for the entire camping trip . . . food, drink, transportation, permits where necessary, scheduling time off, babysitters, proper clothing, sleeping bags, first aid, hygiene, toilet paper, plates, cups, eating ware, recreation . . . you name it . . . because I wouldn't . . . they were on their own. And guess what . . . it was to be for 10 days in June. I was totally amazed at the generosity of the Swakop people, once they understood the plan.

"Love your neighbor" . . . was going to be put to a real test . . . every racial, language, tribal theme was represented, and we will all stay inside one KRAAL with all provisions as if living on a desert island at the Ugab. The Kraal is for tourists built and managed by and NEAR the Village. Each group will be assigned a specific educational project.

They will teach the villagers about the brand new Social Security System adopted by the Namibian Government. They will do the same for new Labor laws, new Workman's Compensation laws, new Election Laws, new Criminal laws, and subject to the brand new NAMIBIAN CONSTITUTION. The hard part will be watching Andrew their chosen leader negotiate it all with Johannes (who I prepared ahead of time when we came up with the idea together during my 10 day Trek . . . We called the whole adventure THE TREK.

Chapter 29

Is there is or is there ain't?

Is there is or is there ain't, my Social Security. The concept of social security was America's first real commitment to, "Love Your Neighbor".

Today, it exists in name only, certainly not in reality. I could take care of the financial needs of an entire village in Namibia on what I receive, but as far as living a decent life in the States . . . NO WAY! I was asked early on by the Erongo Region Governor, when the Namibian Social Security law passed, to be at the Erongo Regional presentation for the general public and to help with the public explanation.

I was called to the front of the hall by the Governor, introduced and explained through an interpreter, why it was passed in the US in the 30's, because ordinary elderly US citizens were starving to death in abject poverty. (that fact alone caused mumbles and rumbles, they could not believe Americans were in poverty). I told them I was born in 1936 and held up my own yellowed old card and further told them, how I would receive this benefit every month soon and it would take care of me for the rest of my life . . . they were truly impressed and applauded loudly until they found out from the next speaker they also had to pay into their fund from their paychecks. Sound familiar?

It is in that same vein with any social/public building or social/public welfare project that will make us all better off . . . the answer is always, "Great! . . . but NOT IN MY BACKYARD", Sound familiar? The simple truth about simple facts on this earth are . . . there are TOO many people and TOO few natural and agricultural resources left on or in the earth to take care of everyone in the way free enterprisers see fit. In free enterprise, some win . . . meaning . . . some lose.

Then, of course, there are the public relations philosophical "feel good" groups that insist, if we do things THEIR way, we will all survive just fine . . .

never admitting it can and will NEVER work out for everyone in society, only the members of their own "feel good" group will receive benefits. Such as, the Sunshine Patriots who love war, the Right and Left wing Political parties who want more services or lower taxes, the Religious cults who want you to live in your bedroom . . . their way . . . or NO WAY at all, ... etc. etc. etc. All pure selfish public relations BS!

I was very concerned about these public issues when I was on the other side and asked the teachers.

Here is my best memory of the answers . . . and trust me . . . I NEVER THOUGHT I WOULD SAY THIS IN PUBLIC. I kept much of what I learned very private for a very long time, the answers I received from the teachers were directed to me alone, not to the general public. Every one on this earth must find their own answers to their own questions and seek their own path to peace.

SO . . . I asked, will this world as it is, survive???

In an immediate beckoning of understanding, I understood:

"All souls and material matter were created at the exact same moment . . . this is what you call, the idea . . . the form . . . the potential, for the physical laws and creative process of what you call motion, time and reality. Idea is simply the plan! Now Tommie you have asked many times, Who are we, Who am I, Why am I here??? It should become obvious to you, but for complicated reasons it never takes hold in the primative dualistic brain and limited consciousness of mankind, that we are all ONE, therefore, exact clones of our creator. Every single soul in eternity is an exact replicate of the original monad. We are God!"

"Yes we souls are all the same. We come to this earth to spiritually test the human potential for all mankind to, "Love your neighbor" . . . for that reason alone, and for no other reason . . . and that is that!"

I never heard our earthly mission put so clearly and with so much common sense. I was going to test Namibians at Ugab in this exact same manner . . . and TOLD NO ONE about my plan!

OH Boy, OH Boy; It gets clearer and clearer . . . .

IT IS BLATANTLY OBVIOUS THIS EARTH IS IN SERIOUS TROUBLE, AND . . . . IT IS ALSO JUST AS OBVIOUS TO ME THE ONLY POSSIBLE WAY OUT OF THIS WORLDWIDE CRISIS IS . . .

Chapter 30

"Love Thy Neighbor!" no, ifs, ands, or buts . . . no exceptions, PERIOD!

Now where have we heard about this very simple survival technique before . . . why from every single spiritual, mystical or religious hero or spiritual writer who ever lived . . . that's who! Why is it that no one ever wants to be the first to admit we are all truly equal, and that, "Love thy neighbor" makes absolutely perfect common sense. It also makes good political, economic and social sense. Maybe the reason people do not practice it is the fear of experiencing the trauma of being the only politically incorrect person doing it? What is it about us humans that makes us so damn ignorant in thinking there is, or ever was, any other way to survive on this delicately balanced planet?

So, with that attitude firmly in mind I decided to do this entire Ugab Trek as a physical, mental and spiritual survival experiment. We will put 20 unknowns who basically hate each other into a survival control group for 10 days and see if they will end up actually giving a damn about each other.

AND . . . I told Danielle, in order to pass the 1st year course with the others, she had to live, eat and sleep with them for the entire 10 days, while I made camp way out of sight downstream. That was a terrifically hard sell and totally pissed her off. I tried to explain about favoritism and its pernicious effect upon any group in any situation, but that fell on deaf ears, she being young considered it another personal rejection and stayed pissed off, totally ignoring the fact that everyone on the Trek already knew she was a half semester short in starting school and were watching me like fish-eagles to see if I would violate my own instinct for demanding fundamental fairness.

The fun part of this plan was watching the different personalities instinctively pair off into functional teams. I did not assign them into teams, they formed them instinctively from their own class room survival team experience . . . they knew the team survival system worked . . . all for one . . . . one for all! They asked Andrew to be leader, since he was anyway!

The teams spread out into the business and political community to sell the plan and get both in kind and $$$$$ contributions, it was a phenomenal success in terms of public relations. The entire Swakop community admired them and soon the Trek shaped into a form with specific plans, then shaped into a pattern of specific behavior expected from each member of each team.

Of course, there were slackers that expected others to pull their weight. One in particular a "Cherman" named Heinz, the most spoiled orphan kid I ever met, friendly, but totally incapable of either planning or executing a plan. This Trek should be good . . . others like him were subtly lining up in sympathy with him . . . now the fun begins . . . the competents against the slackers . . . just like in real life HUH!

Transportation was going to be the most critical problem, one lady had to bring her youngins, the youngest still nursing, vacations were rearranged, replacements at jobs found and other responsibilities rearranged. They were totally committed to getting the Trek done at any price or personal inconvenience to themselves . . . that attitude alone served to convince me they all passed the test so far. I was loving it . . . . people can change, they were proving it right in front of my very own eyes!!

Finally the day of the Trek, everyone assembled at my flat, anticipation was high, one team led the way . . . others in a caravan behind . . . with prearranged pit stops to check on the progress of chancy vehicles . . . and all had that problem. I got started early to be the first to arrive in order to set up my camp site first and then watch them organize. Earlier in the month, I was visited in Swakop by my old buddy Jim Stevenson from Delaware, after a few nice days together where he met all the students he gave me a bundle of cash to help with the Trek. I in turn, right in front of him, gave another guy who was spending a lot of camping time at Ugab $3000.00 Namibian (about 500 US) to give to Paul the manager of the Trust to place the down payment to pay for the Kraal space and other expenses as a reservation. The actual cost per person was $10 N per day for 10 days for 20 students . . . do the math . . . the $3000 N advance was plenty.

I picked the largest kraal closest to the village, shower and toilets and directed the vehicles to park in a row next to the rock wall to heaven. Other than that, I stayed out of the fray. They looked like the Keystone Cops getting their selves organized inside the kraal . . . who sleeps next to who . . . it was a total mess. Andrew finally stepped in and ordered everyone to settle down and pick a spot by the fence inside the kraal on the sand, then he let the woman with children have her choice of space no one objected. Hummmm, are we beginning the Trek by making exceptions to rules or were they just being fair by instinct.

The first major decision surprised everyone, including me. I wondered who would take charge of cooking. A large loud mouthed Afrikaner took immediate charge of the process with “you fookers cain’t cook wert a shit”, he started collecting fire wood, piling it just right in the fireplace (braii) in the back of the kraal away from all the sleepy things, yelling at Heinz, “go fetch some dis size and git to it or ya don’t git to eat a twit “, hummmm, a leader, a bully, or a socially shy avoid-er!

Others milled around silently confused by nothing to do; and no one to take care of, or obey. I wanted desperately to stay and watch the fun. I kissed Danielle in front of all the others to prove my love and loyalty then said "I will see you all in the evening . . . call me for dinner" . . . and left for my place of bliss!

Chapter 31

BUT . . . WILL LOVE WORK?

OK lets all think like bush warriors . . . let's think it through together. What causes the basic physical tensions in each of us? Hunger, thirst, need for sleep, temperature control, elimination of waste, are among the most important and are absolutely necessary for personal survival anywhere. When two or more of us are gathered together a plan must be made if gender, age, physical condition, is a problem for anyone, this principle operates as the first logical set of exceptions to be exempted from equality of distribution of work or task allotment system.

Now add to this fiery mix, unfamiliarity with territory, confusion over language and unfamiliar social boundaries. Add in a strictly confined living space, limited food supply, no leadership or direction and see what that does for creating total social and political chaos. I loved it.

For days afterward, they actually thought they were actually free. They commented about it over and over at our first dinner hour, how wonderful it was. No one seemed to notice from the very beginning, ORDER was organized and enforced by our cook, and chores for cleaning up afterward were assigned by him, he was an instinctive leader masquerading as a bully, he loved the job, was good at it, made an effort to please everyone as much as possible without complaint . . . and best of all . . . he drove Heinz totally nuts with a constant stream of orders. (To the quiet pleasure of the rest of the group)

Andrew and several others brought guitars . . . the music at sunfall with the banked campfire smoke and smells was very romantic and smolderingly delicious. We joked around, told stories about each other and I gave a Zazen to relax the fears of those not used to the bush sounds. We agreed to settle down for the night. I hated to say goodnight to my dear little Danielle, she would never get over that really stupid trick I pulled on her on behalf of my idealism about fairness. But, I knew damn well not to mix my personal sex life into this already smoldering chaos . . . married or NOT!!!.

I awoke next morning smelling the last embers of my dying campfire and sat up to see them through the trees trekking off in the single file down the Ugab River Bed elephant walk, all laughing, joking and pushing each other around like family . . . Johannes and Andrew in the front of the line . . . . OORAH!!!

Things went well everyone was relaxing from the civilization they left behind. I had no idea I was introducing Africans to Africa. They loved the outdoors, the primitive digs, and started getting into it.

The fourth day Andrew came up to my campfire in the early morning. "Sensei, we are running short of food". "Good", I said, "the Trek starts today . . . go back and call a meeting to figure it out"

I walked to the kraal a few hours later and was stunned to see them all working at a some job, collecting wood, carrying water, some taking inventory, the ladies sharing recipes with the cook to stretch compatibles, it was "Love your neighbor . . . heaven"

Heinz was playing his guitar. Andrew ordered him to, so he would be out of the way and quiet. They were a team now . . . no longer a fake family as a temporary psychic defense, but a true tribal team, with tasks for each to show personal worth within the pecking order . . . even the wee ones had a job taking care of Danielle (wink) while Mom took a well deserved break . . . they were awesome together and it only took 4 days to bond through NECESSITY.

What will keep them bonded emotionally . . . nothing . . . except THREAT of extinction of the tribe. When a bonded tribal member senses threat, that person reacts the same as in a flock of birds . . . which all seem go into the air in the exact same instant in the same exact direction . . . knowing by instinct, the proper direction and distance to keep from each other, so as not to get separated and lost and; also so not to be to close as to extinguish each other's allotted space and energy, and never be so late as to not be able to escape with the unit. With their newly found unconscious tribal survival instincts, this tribe will be able to survive any surprise attack from any direction. They were bonded as one.

Chess tournament games began to fill boring afternoons, naps were coordinated, trips to the quarry for swimming were arranged, cooking assistants volunteered in preparing stuff for the cook, showers were coordinated, toilets cleaned, things were coming together . . . we were surviving as a tribe. The village instruction projects were going great guns . . . "more, more", begged Johannes. Then on the 7th day we had our first real threat.

Chapter 32

"Admissions"

Any lawyer worth their salt knows . . . **Admissions against interest** . . . are the best evidence of truth in a sworn statement . . . they are called self condemnation principles by shrinks and addiction pros . . . meaning you can rely on this type admission as the most accurate information available about any person because, there is nothing to gain by saying the bad words against himself with everything to LOSE.

ERGO . . . YOU CAN BELIEVE IT!

In that spirit, first and foremost . . . I AM NOT A PSYCHIC . . . GOT THAT . . . I NEVER HAVE BEEN, and WILL NEVER BE. I am not any type of spiritual impersonator or pusher for GOD . . . I am not on a mission . . . I am just telling you about my journey in Africa. The time comes when a writer must tell an audience which I have come to rely upon as friends, the whole truth . . . OK . . . so please view this next part of my story with patience and try to understand I was totally rejected by EVERYONE I KNEW IN AMERICA for these happenings and I DO NOT WANT TO TALK MUCH ABOUT IT . . . but for you my warrior friend . . . here goes . . .

Where can I possibly begin . . . I was training hard for the Nationals in USA Judo. I was attacked from the side by my heavyweight training partner at our dojo in Ocean City N. J. under Sensei Dick Walters, who trained in Japan for six years and became a world class player and International Judo Champion, my knee snapped loudly and was broke . . . I hobbled, it did not hold, I fell. Dick turned white and ordered me off the mat and to a medical facility. I was reluctant, I would miss training and the contest, I said I was OK because it only wobbled like a noodle from the knee down. I could fight one legged. He did not smile!

Two weeks later after being wrapped in a black rubber bicycle tire so I could go to work and Judo practice I almost lost it from gangrene. I had an emergency operation, Dr. Axe fixed it and told me I would be lucky to walk normal again. I was recovering at home in my back yard when I saw this old lady neighbor of mine peeking out at me from behind a curtain next door; as I was hopping around the yard with large stones in both hands, trying to hop up steps on one bad leg. That's my first actual memory of Jane.

I waved to her every day as she watched my pain in the struggle clapping her hands like a high school cheer leader every time I made it up a step and I improved every day by showing off for her. Eventually I went back to training in Ocean city NJ and trained with a leg brace on. I won the Nationals and after the awards cermony I compulsively drove home to Delaware from Pittsburgh all night in driving storms to arrive early am at her door step. I proudly brought the 1st place trophy straight home to her . . . not to my wife . . . not to my kids . . . not to me . . . but, to HER. She kept it proudly on her mantle.

Eventually, I got to meet and know her 96 year old father, a month later, he died . . . I was the last to see him alive. I visited St Francis Hospital to say goodbye, he grabbed my hand looked me in the eyes and said "Take care of Jen", **I said a sacred YES**, "I will" and he died in front of me. NEVER DO THAT . . . UNLESS YOU TRULY MEAN IT!

I started visiting her for a while to say, "Hello", then started sitting and talking, she was in a wheelchair most of her 75 something life. She had polio at age 13. After the early iron lung experience and trips to Warm Springs at the same time as Roosevelt, and a life of constant physical therapy she could wheel herself around. Her Dad took care of the home maintenance, food and other details, she slept on the couch in the front living room and could wrestle herself on to it from the wheelchair with no help. He always called her Jen, she was Jane to everyone else.

She now had to take care of all her personal details and did quite well living all on her own. I grew to admire her for just that reason and we became chess friends, then one day . . . Elwood Babbitt, my very close friend, a well known and very famous channel called me. "Hey Marine, get the book Many Lives, Many Masters", and hung up. He was my mentor for a strange activity called channeling . . . he used the same self hypnosis technique I explained earlier, used by Edgar Cayce "The Sleeping Prophet" of Virginia Beach.

When Elwood was in trance he spoke out loud as an actual long passed entity. Freaky stuff when you don't understand it. I bolted to the bookstore, bought one and read all night . . . next day I went next door and said, Jane how would you like to be hypnotized," OF COURSE" she said delighted. I told her absolutely nothing else, and she struggled to the couch.

Now before I tell this part of the tale I admit, I was not ignorant of this Shirley McLain type spiritual concept and not afraid of the project, I was a hypnotist for many years, have read every ancient book in spiritual libraries except for the Vatican, immersed myself in new age, cursillo, Asian religions, Masonic, cults, etc . . . I read everything and anything . . . I was always curious about God, so I was not ignorant . . . like most of my general audience was . . . . at that particular moment in time.

During our first few sessions I relaxed her and started taking her back slowly in age regression to the time when she could actually walk at age 12 . . .

and in the hypnotic dreams I had her do strenuous physical exercises that helped her legs and the circulation below her waist. (although she never moved a twitch) She and her doctor both loved it, he wanted me to write an article for the medical journal describing the healing process.

One time when she awoke she felt so good she swung her legs over to the floor and tried to stand . . . nothing below her waist ever worked and the disappointment on her face gave me a tremendous idea . . . screw it . . . let's go to a past life when she knew she could walk and see if she can move her legs in trance. Eventually under hypnosis in another life on local public TV, she kicked her legs into the air on live television, the entire staff gasped.

We agreed to record each past life session like the shrink did in the book Elwood suggested . . . I was excited, so was she . . . next day we launched . . . . After my usual introductory process, 8 7 6 5 4 3 2 1 . . . When I saw her body let go and she was asleep, "Ok Jane go directly to a past life where we both served together". A long silence, I was white-knuckled on the arms of the chair waiting, suddenly as casual a voice as you ever heard . . .

"I'm Clearwater", in a high lilting sweet sounding American Indian accent. It totally blew me away. It was the first lifetime she remembered where we served together in an primative and unknown Indian village in north America . . . She was an adopted daughter and I was the chief . . . and she remembered it while she was totally out cold.

In the next day session, She immediately went to another life as my mother in Japan back in the 1600's where I was a well known Martial arts specialist and was the Shogun's chief instructor for Samurai; (I looked at the trophy on the mantle as she spoke of the samurai experience) and so it went on and on sharing lives together between us for many many years, in all kinds of different roles.

I assure you, she had absolutely NO memory of the sessions when awakened, either slowly or by surprise. I tested her fiercely to see how she got her information when in trance and never told her my plan in advance before any session. One day by total surprise a Master came through, I had no idea what was happening and was told to "be still and listen" . . . I did . . . I was given the answers to questions I begged to know for years . . . When I was in the other side consciousness in Caprivi, I asked the Teachers the same questions and the answers were exactly the same . . . I am telling you that is the truth.

I let her listen to a few of the tapes eventually so she could hear her many different voices, accents and the absolutely un-imitable voice of the Master. She laughed at the different difficult to imitate vocal accents and syntax of the sounds coming from her own mouth. I eventually wrote and published a book about it . . . "Goin for Gold" . . . It was awful, and I took quite a bit of intellectually retarded crap from my family, sunshine friends and foes alike as, "He's CRAZY, he talks to ghosts".

Today channeling and reincarnation therapy is considered main stream everywhere . . . but I was the odd man out in the old days of the 80's and my family and friends rejected me brutally for my creative instinct, broad based reading and native intelligence: and by doing so; declared their own personal bias, intellectual weaknesses and palpable ignorance. I finally had just about enough of everyone's critical horseshit. I quit practicing law and quit everything else. I planned my escape from my marriage, my mushy-headed friends and the disgusting middle class phony religious and personal values.

It took a few long years but . . . It worked . . . in '93 . . . I landed in Windhoek Namibia.

so . . . That's the story about my friend Jane!

When I left for Africa, I promised her faithfully, she would never die alone in that ratty old house, no old ladies home for her either. not my friend Jane. Somehow she found me everywhere in Africa when I was near a phone, she always called on a Monday night and we did the same reincarnation therapy on the phone long distance. I never admitted that fact to a soul until I typed these words tonight.

One Monday night at the flat, a neighbor called from Delaware, "Jane fell, she is in the Wilmington Hospital" I arrived late Thursday night at Philly Airport. found the secret place under the pot for the not so secret key and slept on the couch.

Next morning I went to the hospital to see Jane . . . I am still amazed at what I did . . . I must have been totally and completely NUTS!

Chapter 33

"My Mother Jane"

I was looking down at my Mother, old, helpless, fragile, ready to die, she needed me now . . . I needed her for so long. She was the best mother any man could have. I was shaking my head like those Africans were looking down at me on the cot in the Hospital in Caprivi . . . thinking . . . She looks awful, she will never wake up.

"Dr. tell me the truth, what's happening.",

"She is very ill, but could last a long time who knows, she has no functions below the waist. no controls over any fluids or feces flow or urine removal, this condition hardly benefits the stomach . . . her arms are weakened from the stroke, she should be in hospice care asap."

"When can I take her home, I will take care of her."

"NO . . . YOU CAN'T, ITS IMPOSSIBLE!"

The hell I can't, flashing my mean ass lawyer look. He responded quickly knowing I really was in the trade, "You sign her out, we deliver",

"OK Set it up I will wake her . . ."

"Jane???" Gently shaking her shoulder while she was laying on her side, my face above hers. She opened her eyes and didn't miss a beat., smiling broadly, "Oh my God, Tommie I was just talking to you, I just asked you to take me home a minute ago . . . how did you get here so fast"

I smiled, "I'm psychic", she howled, rolled over, and energetically sat up!.

The Doctor was amazed at her physical reaction to me. "Here are the papers . . . we will have her at the back door of her residence late in the afternoon near dinner time . . . be prepared, my young bull headed lawyer friend, for a very trying emotional time . . . and . . . good luck."

The ambulance pulled up and they carried her on the stretcher in through the back door . . . "where do you want her . . . I looked around . . . saw the wheel chair . . . over there OK"

Jane and I just starred at each other for a long moment not speaking, after thanking the wonderful EMS dudes. I panicked. I didn't want to show fear. What the hell can I do now. She tried to get on the couch and had NO STRENGTH in her shoulders and arms and she weighed a ton, most of it in her rear . . . I couldn't lift or move her. I thought toilet??? Damn . . . she can't get on the toilet . . . . call Jimmy.

Jimmy Cunningham, a reliable old good buddy from my past Union organizing business at DuPont Edgemore.

"HELP!!!"

"I will be right over", no hesitation . . . Jimmy was a real friend . . . he dropped everything and in 10 minutes knocked on the front door . . . "what's happenin Jane", hugging her.

First we found a toilet to sit her on while we worked . . . "one was downstairs" I was informed by our invalid know it all hostage . . . we all laughed. Jimmy got it. We lifted her up by both the arms and legs, then sat her on it. We went up stairs to look around. saw a single bed, tore it down, rebuilt it in place of the couch, found a sheet of plastic in the cellar for a bed wetting cover and plopped her into the bed like a sack of spuds with a 1 2 3 plop . . . . OORAH!

We chatted, he left. I freaked out totally . . . went into the kitchen and cried my heart out. I did not want her to hear so I turned on the water in the tap and pretended to wash dishes . . . WHAT THE HELL WAS I DOING???THIS PROVES I'M NUTS. I don't even have diapers.

I glanced at the mantle saw the Judo trophy and a flash of memory of her constant loyalty to all I am or ever will be awoke me into reality . . . I freakin had to do this . . . I made a sacred promise. I gave her a Zazen to relax her and when she was in deep hypnotic sleep . . . I asked to speak to ANYONE.

(I have no clear memory of the exact conservation but this is a pretty close shortened version.)

"Please help me, some one PLEASE, I am panicked, I failed, I am not able to keep this sacred YES" . . .

sniffling, "I am in way over my head, I beg to be relieved of this burden . . . I beg you PLEASE . . . I cannot do this", crying very hard, "I miss talking to you so much . . . I need to talk . . . . PLEASE HELP ME!"

My emotions were exhausted, the silence was awful, then the familiar voice so beautiful and incredible, suddenly the Master voice spoke out of Jane's sleeping mouth,

"Tommie we are all equal and pick our own moment of death, it is not written in stone.", "be patient with your own inner strength, you have more than you know and are totally prepared for this chore you selected for yourself, we will never allow anyone to accept more than can be carried" "we can tell you this truth, she will pass soon, she has chosen that already and needs only a few months to finish her wishes in this mission . . . we will be very surprised if she stays beyond the third week of June" . . . and abruptly said, "we are finished now, do not contact us again . . . we wish you well and want to remind you, we are always with you, we will stand by you and love you in all your efforts". I never spoke to that voice again, . . . ever. From therein, Jane and I practiced dying.

The rest of the organizing was routine, buying diapers, pads, getting the hospital bed into the dining room, so she could watch Jeopardy, changing diapers twice a day, cooking all the meals, putting up with the cleaning ladies and everyone else who implied in every conversation, "SHE SHOULD BE IN A NURSING HOME" . . . but I took two hours a week off to go to the YMCA and did some serious politicking by phone for a guy running for Governor of Delaware . . . The Honorable, Speaker of the House, Terry Spence, that kept me sane, I met a guy who goes by the name Jud Bennett, the Sussex County Chair of the Spence for Governor campaign . . . . OH and I FORGOT TO TELL YOU ABOUT DANIELLE . . .

More later from . . .

TOMMIE LITTLE. FORMER STATE REP, LAW TEACHER, JUDO MASTER, FORMER MARINE, ADVENTURER, AND WRITER, about his experiences in Nambia.

Jud

Chapter 34

The Light Went On At Ugab

When we were arriving at Ugab, Paul was friendly but distant. Since my last meeting with him, he had convinced an NGO to finance and construct a solar panel system in his river stone house and they were also financing and building an upstairs for himself to live in under the pretense that downstairs would house tourist sales and act as a storage point for goods made in the bush by local villagers.

He gave me a tour . . . it was creative and well built, had an indoor shower, but obviously expensive. A young red headed European girl was living there with him and he acted shy about it. Many tourist ladies find a way to hang on to their dream of being a primitive by hooking up with a bush guy, they don't last long, she wouldn't either. He was a total pain in the ass with women.

The electrical contractor was from Swakop and I knew of him. He showed us the two solar panels and the four car batteries that was the guts of the project, however he had strung an electric wire on a line across the entrance of the Trust with one electric bulb hanging from it. No one in the village had ever seen an electric light. They saw head lights, flash lights, lanterns, camping stuff . . . YES . . . but no light bulb hanging from a wire.

He set up the demonstration of LIGHT from SUN on the evening of the fourth day at the exact moment of the drop of the sun behind the wall of rock . . . all gathered, The SUN dropped . . . . THE LIGHT WENT ON . . . . uhhhhssss and awhhhhhhsss. Frankly, that was an extremely sad memory moment for me . . . I teared up . . . civilization was creeping into the bush and it would all be over soon . . . what a shame, I sensed it in the others as well. It was pensive and quiet around the campfire that night.

I instructed Andrew that night that I would try to explain the LIGHT from SUN phenomenon they witnessed if he would translate to the village leaders . . . he agreed. I got them to focus on the sun growing a tree and the tree turning into firewood then into fire. I explained with words and comical gestures how the trees were storing the sunshine, and how lighting a fire released the sunshine from the firewood for light to see in the dark and heat to cook . . . it worked . . . they understood the solar panels were the leaves on the trees and the batteries were the wood of the tree, and the electric LIGHT became the fire and heat. It took a while but it actually worked. I loved it when the LIGHT went on . . . all nodding their heads YES . . . with the positive sound . . . . Uuooohhhhh . . . Madala!

At Sikosinyana in Caprivi I taught about the tiny AIDS virus in the bloodstream and then how it was transferred through the penis by sexual contact by using the many stars at night as the virus in the bloodstream . . . GOD I love Africa . . . everything is so damn simple. I knew the story worked when the girls would not sit next to the boys after the lesson.

Paul became more and more distant as the days went by peacefully and actively, then he became outright hostile to the campers and me. At first I could not figure out why . . . can YOU???

It's a simple answer, we taught the villagers about their personal rights under the protection of the Namibian constitution, and they wanted to know more about Social Security and Workman's Compensation especially when told they get health benefits when gored by a Rhino and such. It is the exact same reason right wingers get hostile anywhere, especially in America. They get caught out being selfish, "I'm aboard, lets shove off".

It is the major failing in the free enterprise philosophy . . . it serves only the lucky few who are either born into or grow up with a competitive edge within the economic system. Right wingers in the US always pretend to be loyal to the US Constitution until others personal rights are guaranteed . . . it is simply pure selfishness . . . . or "WHO's OX is being GORED" . . . . EE GADDSSSS Paul . . . grow up and get a real life will ya!

By the 7th day Paul had enough of free enterprise democracy and constitutional government. After a few beers in his kraal, he stomped downstream to my evening campfire, and confronted me in front of my father in law, Jim Stevenson, and a few other visitors who arrived that day and saved the food situation, "Get the F*** off my property and take your F****** tribe with you . . . RIGHT NOW"

I stood, smiled and said, "Try and make me DUDE", posing in a comical martial arts kind of way, thinking he was joking. He went off violently spewing expletives faster than the speed of sound about $$$$$$$$$$$$ and how we were all getting a free ride from his Trust. I reminded him in front of witnesses about the three thousand paid a month ago . . . he said, "He could give a damn, the price went up". Wow, he finally triggered my adrenals. He would make a dandy right wing free enterpriser, wouldn't he . . . HUH!

When I was convinced he was serious, I told him I would rather fight it out now, "MAKE ME MOVE . . . YOU BIG MOUTH AFRIKANER ASSHOLE". I gave him the US MARINE finger salute and dared him to touch me. He backed down, I won the moment . . . he was totally freaked out and stomped off threatening something or other. He must have totally forgotten he had no political power nor political enforcement mechanism to back up his ridicules threats, I had my two fists to back up mine.

As much as he ranted and raved he could never enforce his selfish attitude on me. Guess I taught him the earth's oldest and most effective political weapon at Ugab . . . MIGHT MAKES RIGHT!

He was such a pain in the ass after the confrontation we only stayed 9 of the 10 days and left, well fed and happy campers. From that day forward at Ugab and all over Namibia, blacks and colored privately called me "Madala", respectfully behind my back and held me up as their protector.

OH, by the way, the red headed European left with us, she couldn't stand Paul one more day, he soon left the dry river basin for another bush gig somewhere, he lost everything he had built in one temper tantrum and I never spoke to him again until many years later.

The rest of the year and all through the next Christmas holiday season went off perfectly well for a boring little town on the west coast of Africa. However, I was one happy camper, then the phone call came in January from the States . . . UH OH!

Chapter 35

We are NEVER alone, NEVER!

I was always conscious throughout my entire life of a second beckoning in my consciousness. It beats me to the punch when I am talking to others and it clearly has a mind of its own . . . blurting out the strangest things. After my last traumatic session with the Master force at Jane's, it quickly became the only beckoning in my mind. I was informed by it to never speak to it again through another person. I was instructed never to rely on it for information in that manner, ever again. I was instructed to practice speaking to myself in a mirror and learn to depend solely upon my own instinct and the plain fact is, the more I depended upon my own instincts the more accurate they became. It is my only real source of decision making today as I speak. I think a question and it beckons an answer . . . it is fun, frightening, amusing, scary, all those things . . . BUT IT IS NEVER WRONG.

Everyone has this particular gift of individual mental competence, but because they continuely rely upon others opinions for answers, the inner voice cannot penetrate their conscious ego's already accepted group consciousness. The real culprit here is **fear of rejection** from the group; and fear of violation of political correctness, therefore, fear of criticism from the group. For that reason alone, I assure you answers concluded by consensus in any group will always be wrong.

I sense this wrongness immediately in all meetings and smile inside to myself at the fruitlessness of group meetings and consensus seeking situations. In the end, they are always about $$$$$$ and money doesn't talk . . . money only controls minds, not the other way around.

Danielle called after about a week into my MR. MOM routine.

I thought this would be the perfect escape for her from a May-December marriage to an old man. I was totally wrong, she wanted to come to America. Jane had been sending me my Social Security $$$$$$$ as a batch of 10 checks predated to cash one each month in Namibia from our mutual Wilmington Trust account that received my Social Security benefit the 3rd of every month.

I gave four of them to her when I abruptly left Namibia to help her survive without me . . . she had three left for $1000 US each. I told her to use them for air fare and come over as soon as a visa could be arranged. She seemed excited to do just that and started calling every week, I called her in between her calls to me in order to assure her she was welcome in America. Otherwise life at Jane's was pure drudgery and Jane could be a royal pain in the ass just like any other old infirm person and she was as demanding as all get out. I slept on the ratty third floor to avoid her constant, "Tom'mm ie".

Never let the great unwashed middle class suggest to you, **loving your neighbor** is fun and frolic . . . it sucks! My lawyer buddy Wil Redfearn was a champ, he came by often and took me for rides into the country in his beautiful luxury convertible. Jimmy the C, as I always called him, stopped by often, as well as, many other old friends. I handled it! The time slipped by . . . and one fine day in May, Annie, my number one daughter and I went to Philly Airport to meet a newly arrived Namibian, her new step mother, my wife of 18 years . . . SMILE dudes, that's how I always introduced her to everyone.

I waited in the terminal, she was white as a ghost, scared out of her wits . . . eyes glazed over; when she saw me as she disembarked, she ran to me and she clutched me and would not let go. It was her first plane trip and first time leaving her home. Annie saw her and was amazed how beautiful she was in person. I had bought several mattresses for the third floor forgetting it was a rat hole and that was her first impression of Jane's after the introductions.

I tried to make her see the positive side that it was not going to last forever, but she was feeling yucky about our digs. I told Jane we had to make a new campsite up there in order to live . . . she had not been up stairs in many years, it was decrepit, dirty and smelly. I called an old friend in the painting business Eddie Long and he began in the attic and created a great large room with a bed, chairs and TV for Danielle and I to hang out in, eventually he painted the entire two floors up stairs . . . so we had a plan.

One Friday morning during the third week in June (right on schedule) Danielle and I lifted Jane out of her hospital bed for some sitting up time on her wheelchair and she collapsed and slumped into our arms . . . she awoke a few minutes later while I was calling 911. "What happened?"

They took her to the Wilmington Hospital, I went in the afternoon to visit, she was in a hallway on a gurney and seemed quiet and content . . . I said "are you ready to die" . . . she smiled and said, "as I will ever be", "I will see you tomorrow", kissed her gently and left.

Next day, late afternoon, in intensive care, I arrived, the nurse on duty said, "She is totally out of it, she will not know you" . . . I said, "oh yes she will", and . . . after an argument and flashing my smart ass lawyer smile, I was permitted to go in, Jane's eyes opened "Hi Tommie I was just dreaming about you." I said let me fix your sweater.", as I moved a sheet around her shoulders, kissed her smiling face on the forehead and cheeks and said, "You can go to sleep now Jane, I will see you later."

Less than an hour later at home, the doctor called "Jane passed a few minutes ago" . . . and that was the end of that! She was never alone one minute from the time I arrived from Namibia. I kept my word to her father. She died with a BIG smile on her face . . . . OORAH! The following Monday I read her will . . . WHO WOULD HAVE THUNK IT . . . she put a BIG smile on my face!!!

Next are the final two chapters from former Delaware State Representative Tommie Little about his life's experiences in Namibia. I hope you have enjoyed these stories. Tommie is now living in Wilmington, DE, is still coaching Olympic Judo, teaching law and is a practicing Attorney. These excerpts from the life of Tommie Little will be titled . . . A Warriors Tale.

Jud

Chapter 36

It is the GOODBYES that hurt the most!

Many years ago, long before I left for Africa, I asked Jane to get a personal lawyer, we lawyers are ethically bound to not represent family or other intimates, I had a feeling she was relying too heavily upon my personal influence and advice. She was a very lonely woman after her father died and easy prey for insincere mal-attentive people. (You get the picture)

I recommended her to a mutual friend and practicing lawyer I trusted Ciro Popitti, he and she alone drafted her legal stuff while I was away, which I assumed included her will. I told her many times I do not want to be included and if I was, I would spend it on a big party or give it all away. I told her straight, "If you ever talk about who you give anything to I will never speak to you again", She agreed and it was truly a real surprise to read it . . . and a very PLEASANT surprise I must admit.

When I opened the bank strong box it was stuffed with stock certificates and other valuable papers . . . I took them to a broker recommended by Ciro, and when the tally was finished. I was a rich man by any standards and had my own house in the city. I bought beds at IKEA for the third floor, computers for each of us, had the house completely repainted and windows fixed. Jimmy the C got me a very used old SUV for 2 grand . . . and I thought I had splurged.

Danielle was confused about her role as an American, I sent her and Annie to Delaware Tech for every computer lesson they offered and I convinced the St. Hedwig's Senior Center to let me teach a tai chi type exercise class to the foogies. I put it together so they could sit in chairs for the whole program and closed with Zazen. In a few months they were doing self defense moves standing up and feeling great.

It was boring as hell. Even the politics was awful, the republicans were fighting over Mc Cain / Bush for President and Spence / Burris for Governor, I hooked up with Mc Cain / Spence and worked the delegates for Terry, as we all called him. We were the outsiders, I love being the underdog. Jud Bennett in Sussex County, was only a voice on the phone for a long while, he sounded like a professional radio announcer, clear, deep, lots of opinions . . . we clicked. Still it was deadly dulls-ville for this African adventurer.

Danielle made the first intelligent move and reserved our plane tickets on the Internet for Namibia, we agreed to leave the last week in November and return to our desert town Swakopmund for the Christmas (summer) holiday. The house was finished and on the market. We bought every convenience gadget and warm clothing possible to think of, packed boxes full and shipped them back.

We kept the second year of the Cyber University alive since I left Namibia in a hurry last February by using internet chat rooms on Saturdays. Andrew and Juanita did all the teaching after Danielle left for

America and they moved into our flat permanently. Things were going perfectly well in America and I had the personal thrill of meeting my new grandchildren for a few months . . . but . . . . all the old middle class phony attitudes were still around and lurking in political and social situations. My old friends still had not read many books worth talking about and their current political ideas sucked, some were still listening reverently to talk show jerks as their prime source of political information, not knowing the jerks were actually paid to hype highly charged political drama. It was CLEARLY an intellectually dead society. The blind were leading the blind BLOWING UP A GIGANTIC ECOONOMIC BUBBLE . . . . and loving it.

Chapter 37

Honey . . . . we're HOOOME'!

Finally after two days in taxies, planes and airports, I could breath again . . . the 8 hour ride through the Namib desert was spectacular, green and lush from the Good Rains, Danielle snuggled next to me in the back seat and was animated about her experiences in the US of A. Privately we were both thrilled to be home in Namibia. I had plenty of money left after giving a chunk to family members, paying off all old debts and opening mutual fund accounts for each grandchild. I had an internet stock account, social security regularly and a mortgage free house in Wilmington to last me the rest of my life. I was one happy dude.

We started over, we rented a beautiful cottage in town, bought computers for home and away at a social/sports club and we opened a day care school for 3 to 5 year olds. English is forbidden to be taught in 1st through 3rd grades remember . . . so . . . I said let's start early, no teaching English, only judo, soccer, and playing on the 7 computers at break time. (all computers everywhere are primed for English)

I had installed 7 computers with all kinds of games and puzzles for kids and bought judo mats for installation in the social club. In ten weeks they could all speak in English. The Cyberstaff of Danielle, Andrew and another Cyberstudent were not allowed to use any other language but English. I drove the bus every morning . . . beginning with, "hands up" . . . as the kids scrambled into the van I yelled it every day . . . when they put them up, I closed all the doors . . . I would get into the drivers seat and yell "Hands down" . . . and then with all hands laughing, I yelled, "Off we go." Danielle and I had no significant personal issues and we were both happy.

Then the CRASH . . . I fell!

I could not breath, my back was in terrific pain. I stayed in hot water in the bath tub for hours for relief. Finally, Danielle and Andrew insisted they take me to Wotan. I had tears forming . . . he took one look and said, "KIDNEY STONE . . . Call the Swakop airport, he is going to Windhoek." He gave me a shot, I flew, the pain worsened, I was operated on.

Next morning, the doctor was sitting next to my bed when I awoke from my drugged sleep,

"I have good news, the kidney stone is removed".

"great".

"I have bad news . . . your kidney is full of crystals and you will go through this pain again and again for the rest of your life".

"What's my options".

"The other kidney is very healthy you can get along with one easily . . . we take out the bad kidney".

"Go for it."

"We can't" . . . "why".

“Do you know anyone by the name of Annie Little.”

“Of course’ she is my daughter in America.”

“She called all the hospitals in Namibia and South Africa this morning and insists you will get infected with AIDS and refused to allow us to touch you.”

“What do I do.”

“Sign here . . .” and off we went to the operating room the next day.

Out it came.

This was the actual beginning of the end of Danielle and I. She was edgy about her lack of socializing, I was edgy about her wanting socializing. We were not sleeping in the same bed room because of the healing process required and the pain associated with it. We acted normal but I knew hormones were flying through her, Her constant talk about wanting children was met with, “Danielle I was fixed 20 years ago . . . I can’t unfix.”

I saw her anxiety, her hints. As a defense, I decided to buy forty acres of prime desert property way out in the boonies along the Swakop River Bed and set up shop as a real proper Afrikaner. Hein said he could build a village camp site from scratch and we began the building process of what eventually became THE REFUGE, a drug and alcohol rehab village camp site and JUDO DOJO in the middle of the Namib desert open to the Namibian public. I was in pain for a long while and not feeling too sexy. She was a good companion but her family and friends started constant pressure to get her to visit town more and more often and it made me crazy. What I am saying here is . . . I saw it coming.

We lasted about a year as a rehab team at THE REFUGE. Disgusted with the primative camping digs she announced one day . . . I'M OUTTA HERE . . . and stoomped off to her parents house . . . a month later, she was living out in the bush in a hovel with the biggest alcoholic jerk we ever had at the rehab . . . I almost went crazy over that when I heard about it. Eventually, as I predicted to her personally, he went off the wagon and beat the living hell out of her.

I reluctantly said OK to her return to the REFUGE . . . but no marriage Ok, I had already filed for divorce.

Then after a few weeks, by a complete stunning world class deceitful surprise, she bailed him out of jail for theft, ran away with him a second time and I knew for certain, her family, her friends and Danielle were all just plain NUTS!

I did not see her again for a long while. Eventually, I met an old friend, a lovely artist who also had a tragic break up with a failed marriage (funny how we always seem to find each other) and we took up a non living-in relationship with a very nice and adult type love agreement. Of course, I was emotionally destroyed from my failed marriage experience, I had Post Traumatic Stress type sadness, I was seriously depressed, I was constantly sick in my stomach. Awww come on, cut me a break, what do you think I am superman . . . I was a beaten down and totally defeated cockolded old man . . . it was the worst time of my entire life anywhere on this planet that I was defeated. I know exactly what you're saying, "WE TOLD YOU SO" and, I respond, "YOU ARE DAMN RIGHT."

Loving your neighbor is a big fat pain in the ass, especially if your married.

Anyway as predicted, she got beaten up by him again, her father had to fetch her this time, she left him, and took up immediately with another first class Afrikaaner loser, an immigrant holiday hanger on from South Africa a pretender with no passport . . . I still don't know how he screwed her over, but one day I saw her in town, all alone . . . she looked like hell, tired out, worn out, beaten down, when she saw me she teared up.

I said come on lets go home, go get your things, your coming to THE REFUGE this very minute, she cried from relief, we got her belongings from her parents house and I moved her back into the long house in our desert village. It was never the same again, I never trusted a word she said, or a promise she made after that, I could hardly stand to be near her when she talked about her experiences. But we both faked it . . . and it lasted for a two more non-eventual years until one fine day she approached me, she was crying as she handed me a folded note she just typed. I said, 'I know what it says", and I hugged her.

"What?"

"You're tired of living with an old man and finally ready to admit it"

We both cried, then I laughed and said . . . "Come Danielle pack your things let's get you home to your Mom and Dad,"

And that my warrior friends was the end of the Tommie and Danielle May=December marriage forever.

BUT . . . . I am proud to say . . . she quit . . . not me. I kept my sacred YES to her parents at the first dinner long before the wedding . . . I promised them I would take care of her until she was able to go off on her own . . . she could get a job now, she could make it on her own . . . OORAH!

Damn, I'm, ready to admit that one really did hurt . . . no kidding . . . I doubt I'll ever make a sacred promise ever again.

After she left the property, the entire staff left for the holiday season and I spent 6 weeks alone healing in the desert. I heard no human voice and had no other soul to bother me except my two beautiful American white sheperds that I raised as pups and the wise and beautiful Master's voice in my head.

From around our American Thanksgiving time until the Christmas holiday I talked to NO ONE. There was not a soul around to talk to or vent with at the REFUGE, only my dogs and my silent partner, the Master force, now living permanently within in my head. It was amazing, feelings of love ran through me beyond your wildest dreams, feelings of contentment, feelings of happiness, I was never actually lonely once, but random feelings of loneliness were exquisite and being alive really mattered, much like the trips to the Other Side and at Ugab. I knew I finally arrived, I knew exactly who I was, I knew I grew up, I knew I healed.

One fine day while as I was bathing leisurely in my desert bathtub . . . I heard a real voice . . . HEY SENSEI! It was Valdemar the Karate coach, he and his son had a big tray of homemade cookies . . .

"What's happening Valdemar",

"Sensei, I brought you some homemade cookies"

"What for"

"For Christmas,"

"When's Christmas"

"Today"

I started crying uncontrollably, I crashed in loneliness, within a week I left everything I ever owned over there and did not stop crying until I got to Philadelphia. I arrived at Philadelphia Airport exhausted, totally spent, mentally and physically down for the count, totally exhausted emotionally, and all I wanted was . . . **my MOMMY!**

I was afraid to make eye contact with anyone during the trip the tears were very hot and very obvious, the customs man looked at the stamps in my passbook saw the time elapsed since my last trip to the USA, looked up smiled and said "Welcome home, Mr. Little" I broke down right in front of the man.

As I came through the baggage section out to the street, I saw a sign being held up in the air by six angels, my two daughters and four grandchildren, the sign read . . .

"Welcome Home Peepaw!"

That did it . . . Immediately I knew I could start over again, they were all smiles and lots of tight hugs. I can do this I thought, I can start over again from nothing. I felt better already,

Kelly, from the front seat of the car as we coasted down the crowded highway toward Wilmington, "Dad, how was Africa."

Hugging a grandchild with each arm grinning broadly, "Piece of cake", I quipped, and hugged them tighter.

Thanks for listening Warriors . . . you are special . . . "I love you all."

OORAH!

Tommie

*** Here is a personal footnote to my story . . .

Since I went public ABOUT MY PERSONAL LIFE first with emails to Jud, then with the writing of this book I am asked over and over again, what is BOK JU KAN?

It is the three Japanese/Chinese characters tattooed on my upper left arm (the one least likely to be lost in battle) and . . . because they were created and understood only by me, it is difficult to explain. I have been trained since early childhood by the fiercest warriors ever imagined to protect and defend. I am forbidden to reveal many of my teachers or their personal techniques. I tested these Bushido techniques through a lifetime in military, business, education, politics, social relationships and sport. I developed a physical, mental and spiritual defense system against middle class mediocrity who all suffer from the same politically correct delusion . . . **THAT ALL THOSE WHO AGREE WITH THEM WERE CREATED COMPETENT AND INTERESTING.**

Now as an aged Sensei, I am free to add, subtract, change, multiply and incorporate learned techniques into my own defense style which is represented by the English words Simplicity, Gentleness and Instinct.

These three Japanese characters are merely a reminder of my personal commitment to my own spiritual Ideal and represent a summary of what we ancients call “my goal, therefore, becomes my result”. I am trained mentally, physically and mystically into an individualized path of knowing the unexplainable in all aspects of life. One incredible weapon in particular I have used for 55 years for knowing myself is never spoken of nor written about anywhere, either in the east nor west. I am surprised, how many top ranked martial artists who lay claim to master status, are not trained in Zazen.

Zazen is simply an ancient hypnotic induction technique where students are taught to enter into their own own dream world, in order to recreate and repeat that particular days physical or mental training lessons in a personally experienced dream, first in slow motion in order to correct mistakes, then, at top speed with no mistakes to imprint it (brain mapping) as a personal electrical/chemical memory trace of the learning in the practice session, therefore, creating and reinforcing a personal BRAIN PATH as a future personal defense system against surprise attack.

When you reach a point of personal satisfaction in your own PERSONAL growth and gain confidence in your own personal uniqueness, instead of risking loss of confidence because of constant pressure of envious criticism from inferiors for being different, you eventually learn to live outside the box. When you live outside the box you must build your own box of ideals inside your mind. Select three ideals that express your desired result as a human being in progress and visit them in your mind as often as possible. Then just name them as your personal style in a three character Japanese summary.

I named mine after many years of practice, personal reflection and meditation on my life, this is consistent with an ancient disciplinary process in Shaolin education. The exact same principle of this voluntary <u>self acceptance process</u> is what the Japanese samurai call . . . Shibumi . . . "consciously LIVING daily in simplicity by choice, comfortable within the one you individually perfected, living entirely within the one you intentionally created, trusting entirely on the one you imitate when in doubt because personal experience proved it works. Without further ado, here's my box of three ideals that I practice daily. I built them intentionally as my personal protection system while living outside the politically correct box.

BOK

Simplicity in living my physical life, like a tree standing alone in the wilderness is a comfort to surrounding species merely by its existence. Simplicity is the ultimate goal of my life.

JU

Gentleness in my mental life, always giving way immediately to any opponent in order to diffuse the conflict, instantly taking away the opponents momentum and empowerment. Then strike back only when necessary and only when the opponent is totally unaware as in . . . JUDO "the gentle way."

KAN

Instinct as a my guide in spiritual life by listening to the voice within in ALL matters . . . NO EXCEPTIONS. Information and decisions from within are always fresh and to the exact point necessary in the moment, including clarity and information regarding our future and our past.

SO . . . I hear you saying, what's the payoff for this childlike absurdity? I say to you . . . you will unconsciously begin to practice uncomplicated health habits. You will gain an incredible focus on what is truly necessary in your life moment by moment. You will develop an unusually sensitive memory as well as pre-sense. You become a true warrior, relaxed and confident in your life style and life choices. You will reveal an unusual strength to accept anything that comes your way and will accept it with humor. If you already live an individualized life plan outside the box thanks for reading this book, since we have much in common, I would love to hear from you.

However, as a samurai, I owe it to you to invite each of you to contemplate this personal message and if you decide to become independent from your current culture group and follow your own individualized path I will be pleased to help. Just tell me what you need to know to get started and I promise I will help you . . . . otherwise, this book was fun to write, it is truly meant to be informational and entertaining, not instructive.

Oh . . . and one more thought. When you meet a neighbor one dark and scary night and . . . they ask cautiously, “Who are you?” You can reply confidently, “I am Oneness, same as you!”

Tommie Little,7th Dan
Shihan
BushidoUSA

Contact me anytime, 24/7 . . .

tommie.little123@yahoo.com